D1516527

LEFT
BOOB
GONE
ROGUE

MY LIFE WITH
BREAST CANCER

Uzma Yunus, MD

The medical decisions and opinions in this memoir are personal and should not be considered medical advice at all. It's a narrative about one person's treatment and does not apply to others with similar diagnoses. Please make your medical decisions in consultation with your doctor.

ISBN: 978-1-729-07081-9
Cover and interior design by Margo Goody
Edited by Beata Santora

*To my children, who are the reason
I keep fighting every day.*

TABLE OF CONTENTS

"When you were born in this world
The world rejoiced and you cried
Live a life so worthy that when you go
You rejoice and the world mourns"
—Kabir Das

ACKNOWLEDGMENTS

I am thrilled that you have chosen to read my book. Since English is not my first language, I would have never imagined, not in my wildest dreams, that I could have the skill (or opportunity) to turn my musings into a memoir. What started as a series of online personal essays about my illness has transformed into a story of life experience and wisdom, of a physician's life as it gradually shrinks.

I thank my editor Beata Santora who led me to the fulfillment of one of the top items on my bucket list.

I thank designer Margo Goody who turned my words into a visual experience that transcends language.

For years my husband, Dheeraj Raina, has insisted that I should write a book. He has been amazingly encouraging and cheered me on from the start. Dheeraj, I could not have completed this project, or survived this long, without you.

Thank you my dear friends and family (including those from the virtual realm) for your help and support. You have prayed for me from the Hajj to the Vatican, in Hindu temples and in synagogues all over the world and I couldn't be more grateful.

My heartfelt appreciation to all my doctors, clinicians, nurses, staff, researchers, and advocates. I especially thank the brave people who participate in clinical trials so that new treatments could be found. Also a big thank you to my colleagues in the Physician Moms Group and its founder, Dr. Hala Sabry.

I remain forever indebted to my patients whose resilience, tenacity, and will to live have remained a life-affirming force throughout my career and cancer.

The unknown is
scary and feels dark.
But somehow I
needed to hold onto
that tiny light
of hope.
It's the hardest thing to do.

PREFACE

UZMA YUNUS, MD

This book has been long overdue. As my late night thoughts began to take the shape of a memoir, I was gripped by the fear of dying. Most cancer memoirs are published after the writer has passed on. I didn't want that (obviously no one does). A certain fear-ridden writer's block confronted me. Of course being a psychiatrist, I continued to reflect on why I am so hesitant to finish this book, and then one day it dawned on me: I was afraid to finish it. Afraid of what its conclusion would mean. Afraid that it would hasten my own death.

As a cancer patient, the fear of dying never goes away. As a Stage IV cancer survivor, it is especially haunting given the dismal statistics and the probabilities. The unknown is scary and feels dark. But somehow I needed to hold onto that tiny light of hope. It's the hardest thing to do.

I am a changed person. Cancer functioned as a catalyst to ensure that I took a deep look at myself in the mirror. For the past five
years, I have worked every day to embrace my reflection even though
it feels alien. Nonetheless, I work to find reasons to love this image.

I have spent a lot of time reflecting. Reflecting upon the life
gone by and what may be left of it. I tackled tough questions about
my beliefs, my desires, and my terminal wishes. I looked at my
successes and my failures and gathered the lessons life taught me.
I embraced myself for who I am and where I am.

The here and now blossomed in a meaningful way and became
the guiding purpose for this book. My hope is that my experience
helps others who are grappling with the unspeakable find their own
guiding purpose.

1

DISCOVERY CHANNEL

It's a late morning of May 2013 and I'm in a hotel room in San Francisco. We're getting ready to visit my husband's new baby niece. I head into the bathroom for a quick shower. I walk inside to be greeted with the rattling hum of the bathroom fan, turned on by the same switch as the light.

They get all this electrical work done and can't get two separate switches put in? How impractical is that?

I ask myself.

I like some light when I go to sleep, but keeping the bathroom light on means this out-of-key orchestra is going all night. I could just admit the dark scares me. It's considered pretty natural for a child, but this fear somehow followed me into adulthood. At home, I always keep my walk-in closet light on. I don't like the shadows it casts but then those are familiar shadows in my own home, well defined and predictable and highly unlikely to move unless my imagination allows them to.

Fear is a basic human emotion with an evolutionary advantage. My psychiatric practice is sustained by fear: of failure, of talking to strangers, of being alone, and—the big one—fear of death. I've spent years helping others manage it.

A menstrual cramp interrupts my thoughts and I think, *There isn't anything scarier than being a woman. I am so looking forward to menopause.* I lather myself up with soap from the tiny bottle.

Next time I'm bringing my own body wash and not using this caustic soda over my skin, I decide. It is amazingly quiet in the hotel room, and I'm sure the kids are intoxicated by some children's programming or the Discovery Channel and haven't noticed that their mother is actually taking a leisurely shower. I assume my husband is reading a news article about world politics on his phone, having straightened the room up. A hotel room can get pretty messy with a six-year-old and a toddler if it isn't kept up. We've been here about four days already.

As I rub soap over my left breast, I realize I'm feeling something I haven't felt before. Or is it that it has been awhile since I actually got a chance to take a peaceful shower? The life of a part-time psychiatrist and a mom who currently hires no outside help can get busy. The previous year had been an ongoing challenge after our nanny quit and I tried to handle kid pick-ups, my practice, and studying for my ten-year recertification exam. Yes, that's what being a physician means. One signs an invisible contract, committing to taking exams for the rest of their life—or is that just implied in the Hippocratic Oath, next to "Do no harm"?

I actually did quite well at the exam, and it was one of those occasions where I had hard evidence of my success—so much easier than reaching into one's self-esteem every day. Although I have to admit, I am getting better at that too. Finally, all these years of psychiatric training and study of the mind and therapy skills were paying off. It would be very satisfying to help one's own self on a regular basis...oh, if only I could find the time!

As my fingers touch the upper left side of my left breast, I feel the texture is noticeably firm. It didn't feel like this before. I naturally give my other breast a squeeze to determine if this change is symmetrical. I get a flashback of my medical school rotation with a renowned breast surgeon who had patients flowing in from all over the country to see her. I think about the variety of breasts I have examined in my lifetime. I know she wouldn't approve of this cursory exam.

The right side feels as it should after nearly two years of nursing: soft and lumpy. For a few seconds, I mourn the loss of the elasticity in my breasts caused by breastfeeding two beautiful children, and then I go on to finish the shower.

As I step out, I call on my husband for a second opinion. Oh this stupid fan! I don't think he can hear me from in here. I poke my head out. My daughter catches a glance, and just like any two-year-old, she gets a rise out of seeing mom's boobies, and then goes back to her show. My son is so engrossed, he misses the "show." Dheeraj, my husband, tracks over to the bathroom.

"What?"

"I need you to check me," I tell him. He looks at me, puzzled.

"My left breast doesn't feel right."

He reluctantly puts his phone down and tries to palpate the area I am pointing to. "Yes, it does feel firm; it's probably nothing, but you can go see the breast surgeon just to make sure." Although he's an MD as well, he knows I won't rely on his opinion anyway.

When a young mother dies, it is nature's most gruesome crime. It claims one life, but ravages many more.

It abducts bits of her kids who will have to negotiate this world, motherless.

2

AN END, A BEGINNING

She was tall, gracefully tall. Despite being born and raised in my modest and inhibited culture, she carried herself elegantly. In Pakistan, most tall women walk a little hunched over. It's the idea of modesty: If you walked tall, it implied you were unnecessarily drawing attention to the breasts. And now she is lying down, motionless, in a casket, with her elderly mother sitting on a chair next to her. Her eyes are closed and the face is pale, the ever-present smile with pearly teeth is gone. Her two brothers stand on the side, sobbing as they hold each other. Her oldest brother looks lost and aggrieved. My mother is one of eight siblings and now, today, there are only seven.

It's a warm day in May 1992 in the coastal city of Karachi, the town I and most of my family live in. Ceiling fans are humming at full speed but the humidity permeates everyone. Women are huddled indoors while the men have some respite in the breeze outside. Some are sitting, others standing. But all have heavy hearts.

Suddenly, my grandmother lets out a scream as she sobs uncontrollably. I could see her grief mount and then recede like waves. The hallway of her house is crowded. People are everywhere—inside the rooms, outside in the yard—but no matter where you look, there's a heavy sadness in every corner. When a young mother dies, it is nature's most gruesome crime. It claims one life, but ravages many more. It abducts bits of her kids who will have to negotiate this world, motherless.

Then there is me, sad, confused, and feeling useless and terribly unsure of what to do. It's my first funeral. I have seen dead bodies, but only in the anatomy lab, chemically treated and wooden strangers. There is an emotional disconnect between the medical student and the cadaver. Not knowing its story makes it much easier to carve it out piece by piece during dissection lessons. However, my medical experience did not prepare me for seeing my beloved aunt pale and lifeless in a casket.

Funerals in Pakistan are a casual, home-based affair. There are no funeral homes there, no business suits or eulogies. There aren't flower displays or big portraits of the deceased. Hospitals do have morgues, but there aren't any separate facilities to deal with funerals. The deceased is brought home for last rites. The fragrance of incense sticks usually sweeps those homes to a nauseating intensity, and large white sheets are spread on the floors for people to sit and recite the Quran. Piles of tamarind seeds are used as counting prayer beads for those who aren't inclined to commit to reading a whole section of the holy book. Those same sheets then double as table spreads (sans table) for those who came to attend the funeral and now expect a meal.

She looks serene in the white kaffan, a loosely wrapped sheet of white cotton. But what surrounds her is emotional chaos. Her children are here. Her son of twelve standing with his dad as the final prayers are said. Her eight-year-old daughter inside with a cousin.

Their mom, my aunt, passed away during surgery for breast cancer.

Khala-jan, as I called her, literally translates to "beloved aunt" and that she was. Her mild manners and beaming smile, along with her soft speech, endeared her to all of her nieces and nephews alike. Also, the fact that she was married to an army officer and always stationed in far away cities made her even more cherished.

She would visit us in Karachi every couple of months, sometimes hitching a ride in the military cargo planes. She was a quiet force and a happy presence. When she had kids of her own, I often thought of them as lucky to have such a patient and kind mom. When her second child was born, she had multiple postpartum infections in her breast. I remember visiting her once at the hospital and hearing vague reasons for why she was admitted. Young teen girls don't get told such personal details in most South Asian cultures, especially in Pakistan where the breasts are private business.

In a culture where women cover their bodies for religious reasons, there is little acknowledgement of the fact that breasts exist. There is shyness about seeing doctors for issues related to breasts and there isn't much awareness of breast cancer as a disease. Bras are sold as quietly and discreetly as drugs on street corners. You won't see them in window displays and men are usually not allowed in these stores.

I have often thought about what killed my aunt. Was it breast cancer, a surgical mishap, or growing up in a culture where she was too shy to ask the doctor about the changes in her breast? What went so wrong that she couldn't get better? She had even gone to America for treatment, had gotten chemotherapy, and done everything she was supposed to do.

I had always thought that she was diagnosed late. From the limited information my mom shared with me, I know she had gone to the clinic with her mother-in-law and in passing had mentioned to the doctor that her nipple felt sticky. That alerted the doctor to examine her and pretty soon she was diagnosed with breast cancer. I have memories of her sitting with a plastic basin and vomiting, but never complaining. I remember her wearing a wig and keeping her head covered with the headscarf. I remember her gaining weight.

She then had a recurrence in the opposite breast. A surgery was scheduled and instead of my mom getting a call that everything went well, she received a call no sister wants to take. A mother and wife was taken at forty six.

My surgical rotation started not too long after my aunt's death and I would flip to breast cancer quite often in my textbook... and I would inspect my breast for anything abnormal.

3

BIOPSY

My biopsy is on a Friday. A warm muggy Friday morning, much like the suffocating look on my surgeon's face when he rolled the lymph node in my armpit within his fingers.

Six weeks ago I returned from San Francisco. Four weeks ago I got a normal report from a mammogram and ultrasound. Eight days ago I found a lump in my armpit. Seven days ago I made a distressed call to the surgeon.

Life was routine when we came back from San Francisco, filled with the usual hubbub that greets you when you return from a vacation. It takes time to rebuild the rhythm of daily life. I prefer predictability, and routines help me feel grounded. My son is the same. He thrives on a schedule, but my daughter with her pre-school pace and personality loves to throw curveballs in it. The first week back from a trip is usually a limping march but by second week, homework and dinnertime all start falling in place. It's like logging back into life, and it takes more than one attempt to get the password right.

Amidst all of this, I had a fleeting thought that I needed to get my breast checked out. But for a mother and a doctor, everyone else's schedule comes first. Swimming classes, birthday parties, dental appointments, grocery runs. However, I managed to get myself to call and set up a time at the breast clinic.

This wasn't my first time at this breast clinic. The first time I was sent here by my internist who thought my left breast felt "funny." She admitted that she wasn't an expert but because of the "funniness" of the breast, I should go see a breast surgeon. "But I am breast feeding!" I protested.

Grudgingly, I followed her advice and went. The surgeon reassured me that nothing was wrong and that I should return after I am done breastfeeding. The mammogram was clean and in my mind I had dodged a bullet. Living with family history of breast cancer isn't easy.

My first mammogram was in my twenties, during medical school, much earlier than what the experts recommend.

Medical students are notorious for thinking they have all the diseases that they are studying. In medicine, you worry about hidden autoimmune illnesses; in psychiatry you review personality disorders to see if you fit the criteria; in surgery you perform breast exams and inspect your skin for moles. It is especially scary to have seen a patient with melanoma that originated in the inside of the nose, only to be diagnosed when it had metastasized to the back giving the patient a few months to live. Yes, that blood-stained booger could be due to melanoma.

My surgical rotation started not too long after my aunt's death and I would flip to breast cancer quite often in my textbook. I would look closely at the pictures, comparing the skin to mine and I would inspect my breast for anything abnormal. One day I rolled a lump, and decided that it was something to worry about. I made an appointment with my primary care physician who seemed equally scared as I showed her my area of concern. She quickly ordered a mammogram. That's why I had my first mammogram at twenty-five. The first in a series of normal mammograms I have had in my life.

After my discovery in San Francisco, the surgeon ordered yet another mammogram. I looked at him and complained, "But I have dense breasts. Nothing ever shows up."

He said, "Okay, for your sake, we will do an ultrasound as well."

I remember the radiologist spending a good half hour examining the firmness I had felt in San Francisco and noting nothing suspicious.

I returned home only half reassured. Why would there be a change in the texture of my breast? I neurotically kept examining myself every week until about four weeks later when, over July 4th weekend, I felt an enlarged lymph node in my armpit. That's when I knew things may change.

And there I was, waiting on the results of a biopsy.

In the hierarchy
of medicine, a resident
trumps a medical student.
I was dying to know
this man's story.

4

CAREER PATH

My surgery rotation in Pakistan included three weeks of shadowing a plastic surgeon. My fellow students and I were in awe of his skills. He was a short, stocky, but good-looking man who was trained in the U.S. A foreign-trained physician in Pakistan is usually considered better than someone who has never left the country. It's a common habit among doctors to glorify this on their visiting cards. A typical physician's visiting card not only has their qualification written as MBBS, but also as abbreviations of all their professional affiliations with the colleges and societies, like a bunch of alphabets in a strange sequence. Many in the underprivileged class aren't able to decipher those, and the common wisdom is, the more letters the better. Dr. H, however, never did that. But somehow everyone knew about his "foreign" training.

During my time with Dr. H, I was asked to follow up with a patient on the surgical floor. I was told Psychiatry was also following him.

At the time, I was ill prepared to handle Mr. Q. He was a man in his thirties who had tried to commit suicide by drinking concentrated sulfuric acid. He was badly burned inside and out. The lower half of his face had turned pink due from the acid and his lips were inflamed almost like a Botox job gone bad. He had several excoriations all over the face. Since he was intent upon killing himself, he wasn't careful as he chugged a canister of sulfuric acid. It dripped all over him, burning every tissue in its path, including his arms, abdomen, and both legs. All his wounds were glossy from the topical antibiotics that had been applied by the nurses.

I had to grasp the edge of the bed to take in what I had just seen. I wanted to turn around and run. The worst were his eyes. They scared me, not because he was disfigured, but because I had never seen such hopelessness in someone's eyes before.

I slowly walked up to him and introduced myself. He barely moved and acknowledged me only with a faint movement of his hand. I tried to gather some history, all the while distracted by questions running through my head.

What makes a person do such a thing?

How can someone lose hope like this? What are the circumstances of his life? Did he think of other ways of killing himself? What is really wrong with him?

Unfortunately, I didn't have the luxury of time. I was there to look at the wounds, to check his vital signs, and examine him for any symptoms of a systemic infection. I need not be bothered with the whys. I needed to stay focused and stay hopeful that I get to scrub in for his graft surgery with the glorious plastic surgeon.

As I was going through the motions of examining him, the psychiatry resident showed up. He was kind enough to acknowledge me but firm enough to let me know that I needed to wrap up so he could interview the patient. In the hierarchy of medicine, a resident trumps a medical student. I was dying to know this man's story, but there was a clinic full of patients waiting downstairs, and I could really use a bathroom break.

The next morning I arrived early at the ward to dissect the long note I expected to find from the psychiatric consult. I started reading: He was the only son of a business owner who ran a hardware store, giving him easy access to the sulphuric acid. He had gradually become withdrawn and uninterested in working with his father.

This is a typical scenario. If the son doesn't want to pursue his father's dream, it is considered shameful for the family. It wasn't clear what Mr. Q wanted to do, but it certainly wasn't a career selling nuts and bolts. One day, according to his father, his son grabbed a can of sulfuric acid dad and drank it in gulps.

Psychiatry diagnosed him as having major depression and started him on an antidepressant medication. I stopped by to see him daily and was glad to notice subtle changes. I would find him sitting up rather than lying listlessly in bed uninterested in the world around him. He would make eye contact with me and smile occasionally. He was looking forward to his surgery. I would eagerly read all the psychiatric follow-up notes and try and remember the terms they used to describe him.

He had the graft surgery and glorious Dr. H had done a great job. Personally, however, I was most impressed by the smile that returned to his face. I did not know then, but I had made my career choice.

From now on,
I would have to live
my entire life tied to
the word "cancer" with
strings attached....like
the ones puppets
hang from...   you can't see them
                   but they're there,
                part of every movement,
               every gesture, every turn.

5

DIAGNOSIS

On July 15, 2013, I hear the words that push me into a new phase of my life.

"I am sorry; it's cancer," he says. His voice sounds distant and aggrieved. His greeting has a deathly echo to it.

He is in California attending his son's wedding and still finds the time to call me. It's a call I had been dreading all weekend. The five words that I did not want to hear—but they were camping in my brain—had now been uttered. There is no going back. The cliché that life can change in a moment is true.

Normally weekends feel short and are over in the blink of an eye, but the weekend after my biopsy lasted a lifetime. During the sixty hours between the biopsy and that phone call, I had already envisioned my mastectomy, chemotherapy treatments, the sickness, my funeral. No movie was entertaining enough that weekend; no company was distracting enough. I was walking towards the edge of the cliff, and I knew it.

I spent the entire weekend reading all the medical articles I could find about the causes of lympadenopathy (swollen lymph nodes) in the axilla (armpit), and the physician part of me had concluded with some audacity that the primary tumor resided in my breast.

My mind was constructing and deconstructing scenarios. I was beyond the phase of "OMG, what if it's cancer?" and more in the "How bad is it?" camp. My hope wasn't that it not be cancer (too much confidence in my diagnostic abilities caused me to know better), but that it was perhaps the least sinister and in an early stage. It isn't easy when you know that a swollen lymph node, if caused by breast cancer, is already Stage II.

I hate having that knowledge.

I want to be someone who is blindly hopeful, thinking that swollen lymph nodes can come from a nail infection and "the doctors just wanted to be sure it's nothing." I want to be someone who doesn't know what having cancer means in terms of the gruesome treatments. I want to be someone who doesn't know that if her biopsy samples sink in the container, they are likely to be cancerous (they do sink).

On this day, I am told that my life would be interrupted for a whole year to make room for being a patient. And that from that day on, I would just have to believe that I would be okay. I would have to look for good omens, that I would lean on my faith more, that I would feel helpless at the loss of control, that I would accept cancer and survivorship as a part of my life. That from now on, I would have to live my entire life tied to the word "cancer" with strings attached. Strong, transparent strings like the ones puppets hang from—you can't see them but they're there, part of every movement, every gesture, every turn.

The doctor's phone call marks the day of my rebirth—to a life of awareness that wasn't there before. An awareness of the darkness that comes with realizing how alone we are and what it means to be born alone and die alone. An awareness that I am willingly going to get cut, poisoned, and burned, because I love life that much. An awareness of how each moment of life carries value and that good things come at a cost. An awareness of the strength that resides within us, the kind of strength that bubbles to the surface only when the pressure is intense and there is only one outlet, flowing out like hot molten lava burning everything in its path, only to bring vitality after cooling down.

I am forced into a battle I did not choose.

> **The doctor's phone call marks the day of my rebirth—to a life of awareness that wasn't there before.**

Sometimes I would reiterate that it was two aunts, not just one. I wouldn't get too far with that because ...statistically I was too young to be getting breast cancer.

6

IT'S IN THE FAMILY

think you always knew you would get breast cancer one day," Dheeraj says.

Reluctantly I agree with this astute observation. There is a part of me that anticipated this, and because of it, I have always been neurotic about my breasts.

My husband has witnessed my breast inspection ritual every night for the last twelve years. As I would take my bra off to change into pajamas, I would look closely at my breasts, inspect the skin, raise my arms, and search for any dimplings. Sometimes, I would enlist his opinion too.

"Do you think this one is looking bigger than the other?"

"Does the skin color here look different to you?"

Most of the time, without even looking, he would say, "No, I don't see any difference." And somehow I would get temporarily reassured until the next night.

Because I had two aunts who were diagnosed with breast cancer, he accepted this as who I was.

Every time I went to a clinic or filled out a health form, I would mark in bold letters "Two aunts with breast cancer." Most of the time the follow up question would be, "Did your mother have breast cancer?" I would say, "Thank God, no."

They would move on.

Sometimes I would reiterate that it was two aunts, not just one. I wouldn't get too far with that because statistically I was too young to be getting breast cancer.

As it had to be, I had dense breast tissue. My breasts were extremely nodular and lumpy, the kind that could hide cancer for years and nobody would know about it. The kind where a mammogram is not useful.

Of course, hindsight is 20-20. After my first mammogram at 20 came up normal, I was reassured. But I kept up with regular physicals and by 35, I was getting mammograms regularly.

Once a surgeon said to me "With the kind of breasts you have, expect a few biopsies in your lifetime."

Her words stuck with me.

7

BREAST IN A JAR

blink and I blink again. This time with the tentative expectation that it would reduce the vividness of the image I am trying to wash out of my memory. It doesn't work; my eyelid comes back to its original starting point with no effect on the image whatsoever.

Medicine is like that. There are some things you see that you never forget. This image is something my mind had selected to immortalize in my memory, something my neurons refuse to let go of, and something my heart chooses to contain even after twenty years. This one isn't of a dying human or a profusely bleeding one, but one of a breast floating in a formalin jar, free of its body, as if weightlessly wandering in space, with no pulls, no strings, no attachments but the fate of the woman it belonged to. A woman who was related to me, a woman who beat cancer.

I am not sure what possessed me to show up to the OR that day. It isn't a good idea to be present at the surgery of your loved one. But I wanted to be there for her. Once she was under, I should have left, but I didn't. I didn't stay in the OR either. I wandered the cold hallway. There were many doors, and behind each one were several doctors working together to make the life of a patient better and perhaps even pain-free.

She was my aunt, my mother's younger sister, who was lying on the table, a machine breathing for her, anesthesia numbing her pain receptors, and Dr. M working his magic.

Dr. M was an intense person; his name was enough to scare a medical student into a stupor. A man of a few words, his skills were beyond perfect. The proof of that was a beautifully sewn scar that my aunt would quickly and willingly show to whoever wanted a peek, punctuating it with "Look how neat the stitches are!" That scar, which sat on her chest where once the diseased breast hung, was what I was anticipating for my future.

I was anxious. Lacking the focus I usually have, my mind was wandering, covering miles and miles, tossing and turning in anticipation, distraught yet hopeful. Every thought would end at that ghastly image: the image of my aunt's breast in a jar. I stole a glance at my breast, the one that might have the rogue cells, the one that might need to go, the one that might have betrayed me.

I could smell the alcohol, feel the cold OR air, the sounds of that machine, the clunk of the gurney, the haze of the lights. I could sense it all; it was waiting for me.

The OR is ready and so is another jar.

8

FULL DISCLOSURE

Just as I was processing the news of being diagnosed with Stage III breast cancer, another storm was clouding my vision, this one involving anxiety about others, the others who are an integral part of my daily life: my dear patients. Helping them is my calling, and I am the guide to their hope and recovery. I kept asking myself: "What will I say to them?"

I had worked the entire week seeing patients before the biopsy on Friday. I was worrying about the outcome and simultaneously overwhelmed by the thoughts of needing to take time off, missing work, and finding another doctor to cover my patients in my absence. But the first mental hurdle was to tell or not to tell.

Sharing this news ran counter to what I had been taught during psychiatric training. The psychiatric community frowns upon excessive self-disclosure; the prevailing belief is that it interferes with the therapeutic process. Introducing personal details may influence the relationship. Moreover, the appointments are about the patient, not the psychiatrist and her misfortunes.

While doctors in other specialties have family pictures in their offices, these are rare in a psychiatrist's office. Our specialty pays a lot of attention to therapeutic boundaries, what does and doesn't get shared—and if shared, then, critically, how it gets shared. Patients can also perceive excessive sharing by the doctor as neediness, a use of the patient's appointment time to complain about his or her own problems. Not too long ago, a patient had said, "My last psychiatrist would tell me what medications she had taken and how they worked for her," adding, "I am telling you, she was a nut!" I cringed. Will they think that of me? Am I crazy to even consider sharing this personal medical matter with them?

Nervous and unsure, I started to ponder justifications for disclosure. I wondered if self-disclosure could be therapeutic in certain situations. One of the reasons groups like AA function well is because everyone is a peer, a fellow in the common struggle. Could I be a peer with my patients, now that I have a serious illness too, one that will always be with me? Will this information be useful in our encounters? But can the doctor be a fellow, a companion, rather than the hierarchical provider?

My health, my well being, and my ability to work are tied intimately to the well being of my patients. With me, my patients build and rework their life stories; they are people who keep me sane and I do the same for them. What do I say to them in light of this life-altering news?

Suddenly, the faces of my patients started to flip through my mind: Jackie is clinically depressed and her dad is dealing with cancer; Tony just got out of the hospital and needs close observation; Tim has such a great phobia of death and dying. One by one I start to evaluate whether they are well enough to deal with the news of their doctor being struck by cancer. Did they need to know? Will I just burden them by sharing?

While facing the worst storm of my life, how will I shelter them from the wind? How will I keep my personal struggle and suffering from impacting my clients? How could I ask them to share their intimate feelings and not give them an equal chance to ask about me? What if I don't tell them, will they assume the worst?

Cancer isn't like blood pressure, only seen with a sphygmomanometer. It's obvious in the bald head, absent eyebrows, ashen skin tone. In the fatigue, the steroid-related moon face, the lack of spirit and energy. You can't have cancer secretly. You can develop it secretly, but you can't get it treated secretly.

How am I supposed to go through surgery, chemotherapy, and radiation over the course of a year without saying anything to my patients? Wouldn't it be provoking more anxiety if I take a few weeks off without explanation and then show up one day in a wig? Wouldn't that be insulting to the intelligence of my patients that I care about so much? Would that be denying them the human interaction and connection they deserve?

What is it about being a doctor that even in the thick of early cancer diagnosis I was obsessing about my patients and how they would feel about my illness?

How will I be the patient and the doctor for the next year?

Seeing my patients is simultaneously easy and hard. I am both the doctor and the patient. A distraction and reminder of my chronic illness.

9

THE PATIENT

have never quite understood her as a person. I am unsure if it's her personality, the scars of chronic schizophrenia, or my shortcoming as a psychiatrist. Either way, I run out of things to talk about.

Our appointments are usually short. They get mechanical sometimes, perhaps a little awkward. She never has anything to say. I nudge her with questions: "Are you looking forward to the holidays?" "What did you do last weekend?" "How are things today?" If I am lucky, I get a sentence in response.

There are times she will comment about my clothes and my shoes. I treasure those comments as they are an indicator of her desire to engage with me, despite schizophrenia. She tries to dress well but purple shoes, red socks, and a green sweater don't represent that intention. She is clean and well-groomed and she never has an odor, something that I am used to working in a community mental health setting. Yes, chronic persistent mental illness and poverty together sometimes have an odor. Much of the time, a lack of motivation translates to viewing bathing as a chore. Nights and days sometimes blend due to the drowsiness induced by medication, so how can one get a fresh start when morning is as hazy as the middle of the night?

She is polite and respectful. She usually stays in the office as long as I want her to. Sometimes she forgets what I asked and I have to repeat it. I am used to that. Sometimes, I get ambitious and fanaticize about changing her medications so that she is more verbal. Sometimes flipping through journals, I look for some answers that would help me unlock her mystery. But my heart knows that this is the aftermath of severe schizophrenia, the blankness and the quiet, the lack of animation and "spaciness." I sometimes wonder if it matters to her who her psychiatrist is.

I can never, tell but I would like to believe that I make a difference, that my care and my interest in her is valuable. After all, that is the most rewarding part of the practice of medicine: the appreciation of my efforts by my patients, my ability to better their lives, and my life intersecting with theirs.

I have worked at this clinic for the last four years. I come in, my mind sharp and focused; I review my schedule and start with the 9:00 a.m. appointment. But today I am preoccupied. A part of me is unsure whether I belong in this office today, having just learned I have Stage III breast cancer. Seeing my patients is simultaneously easy and hard. I am both the doctor and the patient. My job is a helpful distraction and escape from my own distress, but also a constant reminder of my chronic illness. I am quietly struggling but getting through the day, one appointment after another. I'm trying hard to maintain the standard of care I always adhere to. After careful consideration, I have decided to inform my patients of my diagnosis. They're aware that I will be taking time off the following week.

I take a quick jaunt to Starbucks for an energizing cup and walk back towards the office. She sees me from across the alley. She approaches me and says, "Can I walk with you?" Puzzled, I agree. She walks with me to the back door of the office, then opens the door for me, saying, "I thought you needed someone to walk with you today."

In the midst of my own collapsing universe, I saw hope. She gets it, my mind screamed. She noticed and understood. She expressed empathy towards her psychiatrist. We did have a relation-ship despite my suspicions. The empty look in her eyes is not indicative of an empty heart.

The psychiatrist in me rejoiced. My life mattered, more than I knew. And more importantly, she may be quiet and withdrawn, but the human connection lives on.

...that is the most rewarding part of the practice of medicine: The appreciation of my efforts by my patients, my ability to better their lives, and my life intersecting with theirs.

Cancer comes with emotional nausea too. The worry about death and dying.

My emotional nausea is as intense as my physical one.

10

NAUSEA

The one thing that chemo teaches you irreversibly is how to deal with nausea. I am someone who always got nauseated easily by minor things. Medically, it means that I have a hyperactive chemoreceptor trigger zone and my brain is just on and ready to pounce. If I had ever drank or smoked, it would have lulled those receptors a bit, but being a good Muslim girl, that never happened. Hence, I lived with intractable nausea for months through chemotherapy.

Nausea is a prodrome symptom—a predictor—of something about to go wrong, a sinking gastrointestinal feeling of unrest, a strange stomach chaos that lingers. Chemo nausea is awful. It stays with you for days. The oncologist's office arms you with supplies of Zofran and Compazine and Ativan, but you have to figure out the exact recipe. I devise my own concoction of how much of each and how often. On Adriamycin, the red devil as it is labeled, I had evil nausea. A constant dread that my stomach felt as if it was in mourning—mourning the loss of a normal GI routine. Chemo strips the entire gastrointestinal track of its lining, and perhaps it's the nakedness that makes it so miserably melancholic. Cancer comes with emotional nausea too. The worry about death and dying.

My emotional nausea is as intense as my physical one.

Nausea has an unavoidable partner: vomiting. The regifting maneuver of the GI tract. In my life, I have vomited a lot. I used to vomit with migraines too. Throwing up does come with this sick sense of relief. It is rather twisted to expel profoundly nasty amalgam of semi-digested food and feel relief, but it does happen.

When I complained about the nausea and vomiting to my oncologist, she said, "Try Olanzapine."

I was floored. "Psychiatric medication? Olanzapine? The medication I prescribe for schizophrenia to thwart hallucinations?"

"Yes," she said simply.

The psychiatrist in me felt wretched. Really, cancer? You want me to deal with this irony? A psychiatrist on Olanzapine.

Yep, time for a taste of my own medicine. Literally.

Thankfully, it thwarted the heaving sounds of my stomach and the haunting hallucinations of cancer. I was able to have some peace. At least for a while.

11

BEYOND CHOCOLATE AND ROSES

I vomit again. I wish it would stop but it doesn't and I know it won't. As awful as it is to puke endlessly, it is accompanied by a temporary sense of relief. A few moments of the storm having passed are a reprieve from the miserable nausea, one that I feel acutely even through the post-chemotherapy drug fog.

I retch and vomit again.

I am sitting in my bed, the kids are fast asleep, and it is 10:30 p.m. He stands next to me patiently.

I expect the vomiting to go on for another few hours; that has been the routine for the last two cycles of chemotherapy. Usually 2:00 a.m. is when my stomach surrenders and my brain is knocked out by Ativan and Benadryl, two wonderfully sedating drugs.

I throw up in a green plastic bowl that I used to wash produce in when we were newly married. It has taken on a new function now. I hand the bowl to him. He doesn't make a face or pucker his nose. He has now seen my lunch twice: First in the carry-out containers and now in reverse. I am not a big fan of cafeteria food so he brought me soup and a sandwich from my favorite deli. Yes, he is just that kind of husband.

He hands me the glass of water which I slowly sip, swish in my mouth, and spit into the bowl he is holding. The rinse does nothing for the horrible sour taste in my mouth and I am too exhausted to go to the bathroom to brush my teeth. He rubs my back and drains the rebellion of my stomach into the toilet bowl. I rest my head against the pillow and close my eyes.

I hear him flush the toilet and then water flowing from the tap. Those sounds seem awfully loud in the middle of the night as sleep and nausea battle it out within my cancer-ridden body. He brings the clean bowl back to me. He sits in the recliner nearby and dozes until my next bout of vomiting begins.

I'm sure that nursing me through sixteen cycles of chemotherapy is not what he had envisioned when we married. No one ever imagines their spouse being diagnosed with cancer and having to live that mutual nightmare. Being physicians, we both understood the mechanics of the disease, but we had little clue as to what actually happens when cancer knocks on your door.

We learned fast. He drove me to every scan, every appointment, every second opinion, every procedure. He was there outside every waiting room. He was embedded with me in the trenches through every scan and test result. I remember leaving the MRI suite after my first one, in tears. Clinging to him, I said, "I am never going back in that thing again!"

"Okay, you won't have to," he replied.

He was there to lie to me when I needed it most.

Love is reassurance at the right time, in the right words. Love is being there through a stressful time with unconditional support. Love is standing at the door of the bathroom, and then wiping my bottom, one day after childbirth. Love is being there to comfort and console.

After my mastectomy and the first phase of treatment, I got weaker and sicker. Before the cancer, the household would fall into disarray when I caught a cold and was out of commission for a few days. This was months of disability and I worried. I worried about how much he could endure and compensate for my absence. Amazingly, he slid comfortably into the role of both mom and dad.

How many women marry a man thinking, "Will he be a good mother?"

He had been a wonderful father, but it turned out that his substitute mothering was even better. The hugs and the cuddles and the nighttime routines all remained uninterrupted. The children were being sheltered from the trauma. He was there for me and for them.

As strong as he was through all of it, he did fall apart once. I did too. That one trying evening still haunts me.

I was going through various diagnostic scans to determine the extent of the cancer. It was confirmed to be in the breast and the lymph nodes but they were exploring to see if it was flourishing elsewhere in my body.

The day before I had a CT of my abdomen. The phone rang and we learned there was a "spot" on my liver. A few millimeters of opacity broke our spirits. The children were in the other room as we sat there holding each other, sobbing. He didn't say anything and neither did I. We didn't need to.

An MRI later proved that my liver was free of cancer, but that day remains crystallized in my memory—the two of us, heartbroken, clinging to each other, trying to salvage what was dear to us.

My chemotherapy had been complicated by a severe allergy to the drug Adriamycin, which meant it had to be administered extra slowly, over eight hours, while others got it as a fifteen-minute I/V push. He would sit with me all day in the chemo suite, attending meetings over the phone and working on his laptop. Sometimes when I would fall asleep, he would go out into the hall or in the car (in the dead of winter) and sit with the engine running so he wouldn't wake me up. Thankfully, he was offered a new position during the first month of my diagnosis. The perk was the ability to work remotely and he readily quit his old job so he could be around more.

He was there to find socks when my feet felt cold, there to bring me my favorite lunch, there to watch the kids, there to tell me jokes, and there with his infectious signature laugh. He was there to feed two kids (aged two and six) and a sick wife who sometimes couldn't lift a spoon.

When we first started dating, he would bring me flowers and chocolate, write romantic cards, all of the typical boyfriend things that are expected when a relationship is young. Twelve years of marriage changes things. He still brought me flowers, just not as often. I always got roses on Valentine's Day and breakfast in bed on Mother's Day, but life was busy and romance was overpowered by obligation and duty. Love evolves with time. Career, family, moves, launching our practice, caregiving for family, and financial responsibilities were all part of that evolution.

Love grows deeper and stronger but less reactive. Sometimes it's not even noticeable, but it's there. It is in the sound of the flush as your vomitus drains through the pipes. It is in the cold cloth pressed against your head as your fever rages. It is in the strong embrace as you scream in labor. It is in the foot massage during contractions.

Love isn't just chocolate and roses. Love is keeping the promise of "in sickness and in health." Not everyone gets to test those vows; unfortunately, life brought that question to our home. My husband answered it.

"I do," he said, to living with a wife who has breast cancer.

"I do," he said, to the possibility of being a single dad.

The vows and the promise that he has honored relentlessly throughout my illness, that is love. I don't know what this Valentine's Day will bring, what I do know is that when the nausea takes over again, he will be standing next to me holding a glass of water and a bowl. That is love.

12

NICE AND NUMB

Being an immigrant, I have spent my share of time in cramped airplanes, sitting still for hours. Oddly enough, this has prepared me well for chemotherapy. Getting chemo feels like being on a plane for a long-haul flight. There is a clear destination, and the journey is celebrated. Even if there's some discomfort along the way, it's still worth the trouble as long as you get where you wanted to go). During chemo, I imagine myself on a plane, and all the other patients are my co-passengers. The cancer center is my airport. There are delays happening and cancellations too (when the white count isn't what it should be).

I have to say though, that check-in for chemotherapy is easier than checking in for a flight. And there is no security checkpoint, just a whole bunch of insecure and nervous folks waiting to get on board. I hate the cancer center's waiting room. It's too quiet. If I had my say, it would have blaring club music and strobe lights flashing, with a big neon sign saying "Welcome aboard and enjoy the ride!"

The chemo suite offers a plane-like chair, in-flight entertainment, and pretzels on demand. The "crew" is there to get you through. The only difference is that unlike flight staff, chemo nurses are actually tasked with keeping you grounded so you won't "take off."

The barf bag is another thing common to both settings. I get easily nauseated. I vomit easily too. Thus chemotherapy and I aren't a match made in heaven. I throw up with a migraine; I throw up with the flu; I throw up just like that, when I am feeling blue. I threw up during labor. I throw up post-op. If only I were an alcoholic, I would have an easier time with every drop. (Apparently alcohol use beats up the chemo-receptor trigger zone in the brain so it's not as sensitive to chemotherapy agents. Is it too late to take up drinking?)

With each "trip," I accumulate frequent flyer miles. I have 11 more flights to go before I reach Gold status. Once I am done with the remaining 11, I hope to never earn a free flight ever again. That is my final destination.

Every morning of chemotherapy, two hours prior to the appointment, I slather a glob of lidocaine (numbing cream) on to my port (access to my veins). By the time the nurses stick a butterfly needle in it, they always say, "Should be nice and numb." A feeling of gentle pressure and they can draw blood from it.

When I hear that, I always think, *Who is nice and numb?* Is it just the port, or all of me? Is being numb really nice? I know that I'm not all numb because you can still tick me off easily by being ignorant or judgmental. So some feeling is still present.

I started chemo five months ago so I should be nice and numb by now. Five months is a long time. But is it? Is it long enough to accept a permanent alteration of my life? Only God knows how long the rest of my life is anyway.

13

LET'S ROCK THIS CANCER THING!

H ey, girlfriend! Let's rock this cancer thing!"

I feel a bit out of place in this exercise class. I had scanned the gym schedule and "Low-Impact" seemed consistent with my level of fitness. I speculate the phrase refers to grey hair, slow movements, and frequent breaks. (They used to call it "Zumba: The Senior Version.") At age 44, I'm far from senior, but I drag myself in.

The instructor seems enthusiastic and motivating. Her well-toned arms with a body to match clearly indicate she does more than low-impact work herself.

I quietly position myself in the back of the class, trying not be noticed. I occupy the spot underneath the ceiling fan just to ensure that a surprise hot flash doesn't melt me into a sweaty puddle (thanks, Tamoxifen!). I try and console myself, thinking, *All these women with hard-earned eye wrinkles, they all know what a hot flash is like. You are not alone.*

They say chemotherapy ages the body fast. I just might be the same age inside as these retirees. The fact is that losing ovarian function has thinned my bones, and I am acutely aware of it. I have not had a menstrual period for the last eighteen months. Still the doctors are unsure if I am in menopause. Breast cancer took with it the hormones that defined me as a woman.

Low-impact is the right choice for someone suffering from joint pain, ongoing fatigue, eighteen months of inactivity, and the physical consequences of prolonged chemotherapy and steroid treatment. But psychologically, it eats at me. I am a shell of who I was.

I used to stand in the long Saturday queue for real Zumba alongside other firm, young bodies dressed in Lululemon. I even had a personal trainer for a short time as I had decided that at forty, I should be in the best shape of my life. After all, forty is the new twenty.

Those days are gone. Now, forty feels like sixty, even seventy, and I am taking it slow.

As we start to move to the music, a thought enters my mind: There goes another one. One in eight American women. One more woman with breast cancer has discovered a lump.

The other seven went home to their families and their rigorous Zumba classes, but one got the terrifying call. She now faces the biggest challenge of her life. I visualize her long blonde hair, so beautiful and silky in all her pictures. I see it falling out in sad clumps. I see her standing in line, waiting for the cut, poison, and burn. Yes they are all treatments, and they often work, but that's exactly how they feel—cut, poison, and burn. I want to hold her hand and comfort her. I whisper, "Hey, girlfriend, let's rock this cancer thing!"

I imagine her reluctantly co-conspiring in our cancer partying. My mind floods with ideas: A pink party should be fun, or an all-wig dress up. She should dye her hair pink, like I did before it fell out. She should wear her best lingerie and get pictures taken before the surgery. She should have some hot steamy nights before the breasts retire forever.

She has to live it up. That's how you rock cancer; that's how it's done with style.

The music continues as we keep moving back and forth swaying our arms. I move a bit gingerly, for I have little acumen for dance—plus chemotherapy has left me with chronic foot pain. I used to love to run, but I can't. I feel some self-pity, which slows my pace even further.

In my mind, I keep telling her, "You can totally rock this thing, you must be fierce." That's how you rock it. You talk to others, you connect with survivors, and you keep your head high. You make friends with fear. You learn that uncertainty is cancer's middle name. You stay grateful even in the darkest days. You dress up for chemo. You sport fashionable headgear. You fall and get up again and again and again.

The instructor is insisting we scream "Fireball" with the lyrics. I oblige. Screaming is good.

"You can do that too; scream, be angry, punch a bag," I tell her. Do whatever it takes to get over the initial shock of having breast cancer. If you need to be angry at the world until you find your bearing, do that. Chocolate, ice cream, or carbohydrates, whatever it takes to get out of that numb state. Splurge on a dinner or watch a great performance. Buy good makeup for your down days. Do whatever it takes to retain a connection with your femininity. Breast cancer launches a full assault on womanhood, and you have to fight back.

Let's rock this cancer thing together!

"You need a theme song," I tell her, something that inspires you to fight, something that gives you the will to live. I don't remember exactly how it happened but "Roar" by Katy Perry became my theme song. It was heartwarming when my friends texted me during the Super Bowl halftime show saying, "Uzma, your song is on!" I roared and roared to cancer, through one mastectomy, sixteen chemotherapies, one ICU stay, one anaphylactic reaction, thirty-three radiations, and countless other aches and pains that are too insignificant to note.

I urge her, "You need to tell yourself, you will survive and for this time you have to believe every word you say to yourself. Hold on to faith or your sources of comfort. Do not become a recluse; you need people to keep you alive."

The beat changes to a Colombian song, and it is mesmerizing.

I get distracted from my thought process and take an inventory of the room around me. There are some who are in their element, others who are just winging it, but everyone is trying to find their pace.

"That's what it is, Sister, you need to find your pace, your rhythm, your beat!"

Most people tell me that I did cancer with style and grace. I believe them. I had to. What choice did I have? Curl up into a ball and complain about life being life? Whoever lives a predictable life? Not me, not you.

Sometimes the pace is fast, sometimes painfully slow. The trick is to keep moving, adapt to what feels right to you, listen to your body.

I start to get winded about thirty minutes into the class. I feel the grief. The grief of losing the strong healthy body I once had. The prosthesis starts to feel cumbersome. I notice the lymphedema prevention sleeve feels full. Against my desire to return to fitness, several obstacles are stacked up.

Once someone has undergone a mastectomy and lymph node removal, there is a lifetime risk of developing swelling in the affected side. Who knew removing a breast can lead to arm swelling? Vigorous exercise can cause the body to heat up, increase in lymph return, and boom! Inflated arm! Another cancer souvenir. A potentially irreversible condition.

I notice my fingers are full, and suddenly the pace of my movements starts to match the steel-haired lady next to me. Her hair reminds me of the newly-diagnosed friend of a friend. I assume she is physically fit, just like I was when my cancer first got diagnosed eighteen months ago. I was training for a 5k and lifting weights. I was fit and lean and strong. Now I am moving snail-like, trying not to exert myself, worried about lymph accumulation, wearing a medical alert bracelet, wrestling with my prosthesis to get through a low-impact aerobics class.

Cancer does its best to take away outer beauty and inner strength.

The soundtrack changes, and I hear a very familiar song, "Jai Ho" from the movie *Slumdog Millionaire*. Jai Ho means

"Let victory prevail!" And it's appropriate here.

Let's rock this cancer thing!

Most people tell me that I did cancer with style and grace. I believe them. I had to. What choice did I have? Curl up into a ball and complain about life being life? Whoever lives a predictable life? Not me, not you.

Human life is
fluid and unpredictable.
Over time, we doctors
get good at maintaining
distance from our patients'
emotional trauma.

14

S/P MASTECTOMY

I have probably written and read the phrase "S/P mastectomy" in-numerable times during my medical career. The S/P in medical lingo is Status Post. We doctors are into status, as in, "What's the current status?" The here and now, the current medical status, is of utmost importance. That's what dictates the flow of oxygen, the rate of the I/V, the setting of the ventilator, all of it. We are trained to appraise the here and now with precision. "Status Post" is the past that is relevant to the present. I am status post mastectomy too. But even though I had written it many times in the past, only now do I understand the weight of being a status post.

Doctors write "Gravida" and "Para" in OB charts. Sometimes there is a mismatch, more gravidas (pregnancies), less paras (births). Much of the time it's about getting the full history and moving on to the need of the hour, rather dealing with the lost pregnancy that the person sitting across from us has experienced.

Loss is an ongoing theme of a medical career. You lose some; you gain some. If doctors got stuck on losses, they would never be able to function. We value the little battles we win and draw strength from them. A baby delivered without complications, a surgery without post-op infection, a patient wanting to live despite heart-wrenching clinical depression, all fuel our desire to fight on. We somehow muddle through the losses. A lost patient life is usually countered by the thought that we did everything we could, or the platitude, "She is comfortable now." Or even, "Look at how many I've saved!" It's an ongoing journey of doing your best and convincing yourself of that so you can move past the losses. Human life is fluid and unpredictable. Over time, we doctors get good at maintaining distance from our patients' emotional trauma. If every time a surgeon making the first incision stopped to think about how much it will hurt when the patient wakes up, he couldn't do the job. It's a double-edged sword of compassion and self preservation.

I have written the words "S/P mastectomy" as a doctor many times. To me it indicated that this person endured a major surgery, has been under anesthesia, has the ability to recover, and has a scar from the surgery. Likely the culprit is breast cancer, which was the reason for the mastectomy in the first place. So my note would document the presence or absence of metastatic disease and current status.

This is all done from a professional distance, but of course, doctors aren't robots. The humanity always trumps the situation. We cry with patients' families, with patients who fight off death successfully. But we are also trained to wipe away those tears and walk into another patient's room, where yet another unexpected emotional challenge may be waiting.

I was recently reviewing the chart of a new patient who I haven't seen yet, but her records had arrived ahead of time and my gaze stuck on the phrase "S/P Mastectomy." I know what Status Post Mastectomy means. No, this time, I really understand what it means to be Status Post Mastectomy.

- S/P Mastectomy means having lost a body part that defines you as a woman.
- S/P Mastectomy means having been wheeled to the OR knowing you will wake up disfigured.
- S/P Mastectomy means taking pictures of the last time you can wear a regular bra.

- S/P Mastectomy means having a seven-inch long scar across your chest and being able to feel all your ribs.
- S/P Mastectomy means always having to wear a prosthesis. Having to travel with it, having to swim with it.
- S/P Mastectomy means feeling utterly frustrated if you can't find your prosthesis because you can't leave home without it. (Well, you can sometimes under a heavy coat, but it will feel off balance.)
- S/P Mastectomy means feeling envy at another woman's low-neck blouse.
- S/P Mastectomy means remembering cancer every time you change or shower.
- S/P Mastectomy means wondering if you are still attractive or still a woman.
- S/P Mastectomy means feeling incomplete when the prosthesis comes out at night.
- S/P Mastectomy means enduring a series of painful reconstructive surgeries, should you choose it.
- S/P Mastectomy means being on the watch out for lymphedema for the rest of your life.
- S/P Mastectomy means losing a sensual zone of your body.
- S/P Mastectomy means a life changing experience that not everybody understands.

Fortunately, for my patient and me, we will go over the history in a way that only few understand. I look over the line again and smile. "Status Post Mastectomy." I know what that means; I really do.

Perhaps soon
I will vacation
on a real tropical
island, without
the "X" mark
on my chest.

15

RADIATION

My idea of relaxation is certainly not staring at a crooked poster on the ceiling of a hospital room with heavy radiation equipment around me. I don't think the hole at the center of the poster through which the red laser is peeking can convince me (or any other patient) that they are looking at a scenic island with peaceful waterfalls. It occurs to me: If everyone believed in the same God, it would be possible to have a heavenly image up there, and then when a beam comes out of the pin hole, it would be more believable as divine intervention.

Honestly, I have no idea what is coming through there. Chemotherapy is something I saw and felt (the side effects made it that much more real). But this, it's completely intangible. I just need to have faith.

Lying on the radiation machine with both hands raised and breast exposed is unnerving. The "hands up" position always evokes a feeling of fear and unpredictability. Our brain is fascinating at making associations and the association of both hands being up is that of being vulnerable. This is certainly appropriate since I am here to get radiation treatment with the goal of eradicating any stubborn cancer cells that may have survived the surgeries and chemotherapies.

The ladies at the reception seem familiar with the crowd in the small tightly packed waiting area. They should be since radiation treatment is given five days a week for several weeks. They know patients by their first names and usually their accompanying friend or relative. When I declare, "I am here for my shake and bake," they crack up. (My radiation oncologist is Dr. Sheikh). They are not used to chirpy cancer patients. The chairs in the waiting room are occupied by people with a depressed affect and sickly demeanor.

Radiation oncology is a topic not frequently discussed in medical school unless you're inherently interested in it. It's usually a department tucked away in the basement of a medical center or in an area that many don't pass through. So despite being a physician for almost twenty years, I had no idea what happened there until I arrived as a patient.

The appointment begins with changing into the dreaded hospital gown. This will be the routine for another 32 days. Being a sucker for unique products, I have acquired a designer radiation gown for breast cancer patients. Unfortunately, it doesn't make the ordeal any better. I am neither more fashionable nor more covered.

I walk into the radiation room where it is cold and dark. Soft music doesn't add much to the ambiance. The black markings on my chest help the technicians line me and the machine up in the proper position. This reminds me of the old embroidery machines that I used to watch with fascination at the street corner as a child. The craftsman would line up the needle on the carefully drawn design and give the machine a whirl. Well, now facing me is a round disc attached to a huge machine arm emitting rays that intersect right at the spot where the "X" is on my chest. I can see my image in the glass. The machinery inside opens tiny metal doors with a disturbing screeching sound. I lay still, with my chin up since I don't want my chin to get radiated. Then I breathe. After few seconds the machine moves, and now it is angled to my side, and I can see the darn poster again.

I am quite skilled at imagery and have taught it to my patients many times. But now as the radiation equipment hovers around me, I just can't summon the power to imagine that I am basking in sunshine on this beautiful island full of waterfalls. What I have gotten good at though is believing that the little energy bundles that come out of the machine are hitting my skin and making sure that all rogue DNA is blasted away one by one. Just thirty-two more treatments to go. I softly pray for the healing rays to make me disease-free. Then perhaps soon I will vacation on a real tropical island, without the "X" mark on my chest.

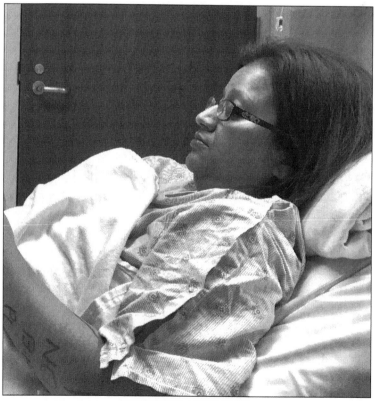

WAITING FOR ANESTHETIST

Long and
highlighted, the
wig was my secret
weapon against the
humiliation of cancer.
I was prepared.

16

ON RAZOR'S EDGE

I hear the buzzing sound in my ears. I plead "Do I really have to do this? I don't need to, do I? Not again?!" I don't remember what comes next in this dream, but I can never forget the sound of the electric razor. It haunts me.

After two cycles of Adriamycin and Cytoxan my hair started to fall out. I had already cut it pixie short by that time. My scalp had become sore which was supposed to signal that hair loss was coming. I remember lying down, in bed, thinking, *It will probably be tomorrow morning.* I had heard stories of women waking up in the morning with all of their hair on the pillow. I wondered if it would be that dramatic or if it would be slow in my case. It was a Friday night. People usually go out on Fridays to have fun and relax. I was in bed contemplating hair loss and what my head would look like without hair. I had already given up a breast; now it was the hair. I reassured myself that it would be all right.

The next day it started to come out in bunches. I called my hair salon for an appointment to have my head shaved. I am not sure how I found the courage to do that. To make the appointment and walk in the salon, to say, here I am, let's do this.

The salon was full that Saturday afternoon, women in for highlights and haircuts and hairdos and updos. Life as usual. They were flipping through magazines as they sipped their coffee, waiting for their new look. And here I was, dreading my new look. In my tote bag, I had a wig I had bought online. Long and highlighted, the wig was my secret weapon against the humiliation of cancer. I was prepared.

Women in the waiting room were planning to walk out prettier than before. My "after" would be the first public announcement that cancer had arrived. I tried to stay calm.

A woman in her fifties named Barb asked me to follow her. She didn't put me in her regular chair but escorted me to a small closet-like room. There was a mirror reclined against the wall. It seemed like their storage space.

"I thought you would like some privacy."

I nodded in agreement. I felt relieved and touched by the kindness, even though I was in the storeroom of a fancy salon. This was the best room for what we were about to do.

She asked me, "Ready to get started?"

I nodded, "Yes."

Then the sound of the buzzer came on and the blade pierced my hair. I saw my hair fall to the ground again and again and again.

And soon enough, it was all on the floor.

My head felt light but bumpy and itchy.

I don't remember what Barb and I talked about, but we were talking. I pretended it was a regular hair appointment where the hairstylist tells you about her life and you chime in with critical interjections. The subject was either diet or smoking habits or that bitchy girlfriend who tried to screw her over. But then there was nothing normal about this hair appointment.

She had a buzzing razor in her hand.

17

FIRST DAY OF SCHOOL

A family is outside, waving their fourth grader good-bye as he gets on the school bus. It's a crisp midwest morning, the sun is shining, and everything is rich in color and sparkling in the sunshine. The parents look tired and a little out of sorts while the kids maneuver their backpacks, wonder and excitement in their eyes.

The crossing guard has arrived and parents are relieved to see the same guy from last year—a cheerful chatty man who waves greetings at everyone.

There is lunch in the backpack and a snack too: carrots with ranch dip. There are random conversations about weather and school that will be quickly forgotten.

The first day of school.

Families are expecting a return to the routine. The pools will close. Activities will start.

As the bus pulls over, kids line up, and there's a sudden commotion. Goodbyes and hugs ensue. Kids get on the bus; it slowly drives away.

Parents head back home to finish their coffee and get settled or rush off to work.

Once home, one mom sobs profoundly. She wails in pain. Her

husband holds her for as long as she cries. She wants her pain to turn into tears and leave her so she can also finish her coffee and pretend that everything is all right. She succeeds in doing that most of the time. But today is different.

She is unsure how many more of these days she will have.

"Make memories." That's the advice of cancer commentators.

I made some more today, and I stay hopeful there will be another first day of school for this mom.

18

RECONSTRUCTION

I am standing with my hands on my hips while he is busy staring at me. I am naked from the waist up. He has a camera—a professional-looking one. There's a black background screen and a metal stool that spins. It's a small room with dim lighting; the camera flash fills it with lights briefly. It's just me and him. I, a stressed-out woman raised in a very modest culture; he, a stranger holding the camera. His coat, the white coat, however, makes this scene marginally tolerable.

He is focused on my breasts. His eyes are scanning me closely; it's uneasy and unnerving. Even though he is snapping away, asking me to rotate my body so he can capture all angles and curves, mentally he is calculating how the reconstruction would happen. He is tall and intense and seems to love what he does.

Never in a million years had I thought I would be doing a photo shoot of my bare breasts. But when cancer happens, all rules are void, all assumptions go out the window. You do whatever it takes to get this monkey off your back and keep it away. You agree to things you would have bet your life were impossible before. You make decisions that send shivers up your spine, and you accept it all with a heavy heart and impending fear. Cancer changes everything.

I had been referred to a plastic surgeon shortly after my diagnosis and treatment plan were established. Through the early phase of diagnosis, what kept the panic at bay was the possibility of reconstruction, a surgery to rebuild the removed breast. I heard from ignorant but well-meaning friends, "You will get new perky ones and you will get to pick your size this time!" (The assumption being that I would chose reconstruction.)

Even the plastic surgeon asked me, "If you had your druthers, what cup size would you prefer?"

"Full of anything but cancer" should have been my response, but I was quiet and lost.

In my mind, the word "reconstruction" conjures hard hats and heavy machinery. Construction, or putting something together, is far from what you want to hear when your heart is still protesting and broken from the blow of cancer. I tried to grasp this truth. "This guy will put me back together, at least overtly."

Recovery from cancer occurs both outwards and inwards, and it is said that getting reconstruction can improve recovery from the trauma. I can see the point. I just don't know how anyone forgets about having had cancer, whether you look down and see a flat scar or a reconstructed lump.

Prior to the photo shoot, I sat in the plastic surgeon's office playing with the silicone implant kindly brought to me by the nurse and flipping through an album of reconstructed boobs, given to reassure me of the doctor's skills and the results I could expect.

Big breasts, small breasts, round and firm, reconstructed, man-made, post cancer, femininity resurrected, self-esteem glued.

I was mentally writing the obituary of my breast as he talked over the options available to me. At five-foot-four and 120 pounds, I was fit and healthy, which (before this whole process) was a source of pride. However, the surgeon was clearly disappointed that I didn't have enough fat in my body to put together a fake breast. That procedure would be called an autologous transplant, meaning that the tissue comes from my own body. So much for being fit and not having fat to spare!

If I opted for immediate reconstruction, my only option would be a silicone implant. I had obviously heard about silicone implants and seen my share of plastic surgery reality shows. "This shouldn't be too hard," I thought.

Of course what I didn't realize at first was that breast reconstruction isn't really the same as a boob job. It's a lot more complex. The surgeon is dealing with a diseased breast, salvaging as much skin as possible without leaving the cancer behind and then putting it together into a rounded shape which has some resemblance to a human breast. That is very different from Pamela Anderson-esque implants, or Angelina Jolie's famously reconstructed breasts that didn't have cancer in them.

In reconstruction, cosmetic appeal is not the primary goal but rather an effort to rehabilitate the patient. Good results are never guaranteed. The lucky ones are happy with what they get; others suck it up as yet one more emotional scar from the plunder of cancer. There are satisfying outcomes, and then there are horror stories. With a recent cancer diagnosis, I didn't feel that luck was currently favoring me.

The pictures I looked at were reassuring though. The chest wall won't be flat; there will be something there. Something to fill out fitted dresses, something that would keep me at least partially complete.

I had struggled with the idea of whether or not to get reconstruction in the first place. My aunt, a thirty-year breast cancer survivor, did not have reconstruction and she seemed to manage. However, I was told that most younger women opt for reconstruction. I couldn't decide. Being a physician did not offer a significant advantage in this scenario.

I called my aunt and asked her, "What do you think I should do?"

Her answer was, like her, pragmatic: "Get it done; it makes things a lot easier. The prosthesis is a hassle, I didn't care for it—

something permanent is so much better."

I heard the longing in her voice.

An implant is really a permanently placed prosthesis that you can't remove at night when you go to bed. It sits on your chest, making it hard to lose in the closet. It probably requires some getting used to.

Looking for more data, I called another friend, a younger survivor, one year out of treatment. She strongly advocated for it, but then she said, "It's between you and your husband." Up until then I wasn't even thinking about him. My thought process was, "I have cancer. They will cut it out. I will have no breast. Do I want a new one?"

Suddenly, I was reminded of the sexuality of the breasts and my identity as a woman. I felt even more confused. My breast surgeon seemed matter of fact about reconstruction as if that was the natural path I should take. I was given information about mastectomy, drains, implants, and other paraphernalia. I was given a poufy fake breast to stick inside the post-operative camisole. All of this was happening too fast. I had just received a crushing diagnosis and my mind was in a mental fog. I could barely decide what to eat for lunch or what to wear to the doctor's appointment and now I am expected to make sane decisions about my future? I felt stressed and numb. I could not access my emotions. All I could do was work through a mental algorithm of pros and cons.

You can get reconstruction at the time of mastectomy, which is called immediate reconstruction. After removing the diseased breast, the surgeon will typically put a small fluid-filled pouch called the "tissue expander" underneath the chest muscle to help the skin stretch. This requires repeated visits to the surgical office to get saline injections which cause the skin to expand to make room for the future reconstructed breast (yes, the expansion is painful). The expander is then replaced with a more permanent kind of implant (yes, that requires a second surgery). A third surgery to reconstruct the nipple completes the process (and that nipple is devoid of any feeling).

Delayed reconstruction means exactly how it sounds, getting reconstruction at a later time. This option typically involves surgical procedures to acquire skin grafts. Plastic surgeons can take tissue from the back, abdomen, and buttocks and put a breast together. They can swing the muscle from your shoulder blade to the front to make a breast.

The advantage of having your own tissue is that it ages with you, gains and loses weight with you, and doesn't carry the risk of wandering or rupturing the way an implant does. But autologous flaps can fail, get terribly infected, and cause lots of pain, both at the reconstructed site and the donor site.

Reconstruction is done in steps. It is not just one procedure!

Getting implants is considered easier than using a patient's own tissue. Implant procedures are shorter with generally faster recovery periods and less blood loss, but they require more follow up visits. The biggest downside with implants, of course, is that they don't last a lifetime. So choosing this option, you're essentially signing up for a minimum of two surgeries in the future.

If I considered an autologous implant, I would have to make peace with additional scars in the area of the grafts. Whether the skin came from the abdominal wall, buttocks, or the back side of my shoulder, it could lead to a weakening of the donor site.

I tried to assimilate all this information. Whichever type of reconstruction I chose would increase the potential for side effects.

The good thing was that whichever option I chose, I didn't have to worry about paying for it. The Women's Health and Cancer Rights Act of 1998 has sheltered women from the uncertainty of coverage for reconstruction. Now group plans, insurance companies, and HMOs that pay for mastectomy are required by law to pay for reconstruction as well.

I tossed around the idea of "going flat." I would certainly be lopsided (a DD cup sways the center of gravity). I couldn't be one of those women who choose to forgo mastectomy and then throw on a tank top without prosthesis and no one notices. My missing breast would be very noticeable.

So I agreed with the surgeon and signed up to get a new breast, which would be nothing like the one I would lose and would be devoid of any sensation (yes, a rarely-discussed fact is that reconstructed breasts are numb).

I remember the night before the surgery. My daughter Gauri fell asleep in my lap, cozily nuzzled between the two soft and friendly entities. There she was breathing softly with her face burrowed in my chest, and I knew that this was the last time she had this comfort. I had to remind myself that I needed to do the surgery so she still has a mom to hug and cuddle with.

On the morning of the surgery, I went to see the plastic surgeon to get marked up. He used a black Sharpie to show the breast surgeon how he wanted my breast excised. Then I headed to the hospital.

I woke up with my left chest in bandages and two drains emerging from underneath my armpit. I was in pain and felt terrible. The details get fuzzy as to when the bandages got removed, but I do remember the first time I saw the "mini boob," the small reconstructed lump on my chest.

I rejoiced, "I am not flat!" At least something is there. I could see the sutures and it wasn't the prettiest sight but nonetheless…not flat. Two days post-op I started to notice that the skin on the newly constructed breast had started to change color. I felt something was wrong and contacted my plastic surgeon's office. They recommended a repeat surgery to "clean out the dead skin."

Four days after a six-hour mastectomy, I was told I needed to go back into the OR. I was devastated. I wanted to scream, "Just leave me alone! Why should I go through any of this?"

I asked the surgeon to remove the expander during the second procedure. I was done with reconstruction. I gave up the idea of coming together surgically. I had sixteen cycles of chemotherapy ahead of me. It was more than I could bear. So I embraced the prosthesis and the special bras and the lopsidedness. I accepted the fact that I could not walk into a department store and purchase a bra off the rack. I accepted that I would be dependent on a silicone prosthesis to look whole.

I decided to go flat because of the series of surgeries that the reconstruction process requires, because of the innumerable doctor visits, the risk of infections, the risk of repeated anesthesia, the risk of implant failure, the pain, and, above all, prolonging my role as a patient. I wanted all of it to end as soon as possible.

When it comes down to it, each person will make their own decision, but it's unfair and wrong for newly diagnosed women to be burdened with such a major decision during the most difficult phase of the cancer process. I especially feel for those women who don't have the luxury of my medical background and are not always properly educated about their choices. I feel sad for those who opt for reconstruction without a clear road map for dealing with complications. This, of course, happens in parallel with other cancer treatments like chemotherapy and the additional, unexpected challenges of those harsh treatments. For example, radiation sometimes causes the implant to harden and become painful.

After finishing sixteen cycles of chemotherapy and thirty-three radiations, I felt done. I was able to focus on rehabilitation because I was not burdened with the reconstruction process. I could take a break from appointments. I didn't feel like surgical work in progress. Time becomes a very precious commodity after cancer. One loses a lot of time during treatment. I was happy to not have to give up more time away from my family and my life.

Another concern I had was my mental sharpness. "Chemo brain" is a known side effect of chemotherapy, causing memory and attention problems in many survivors. Repeated anesthesia on top of that could be more impairing. It's not clearly known or studied but I didn't want to find out.

Breast amputation (whether followed by reconstruction or not) is a traumatic experience. It's hard to know whether to let go of the breast completely or try and salvage something from this grand theft of femininity. I recently got scanned and measured for a custom prosthesis that will be made to look exactly like my other breast. That feels good enough. That feels right for me. Whatever one chooses, the decision will always be difficult and stressful. I opted out and am happy with my choice.

In Loving Memory of Lt. Colonel Mammary G.

It is with great sadness that we report the unfortunate demise of Lt. Colonel Mammary G. on August 8th, 2013 at the University Hospital. The services of the Lt. are acknowledged and regarded by those who knew her well. Besides performing with aesthetic valor for a number of years, the Lt. served two tours of lactational duties in 2007-2008 and then again in 2011-2012, receiving honorable discharge both times. The Lt. will be recognized with the highest honors and a silicone trophy will be erected at her gravesite. She is survived by her twin, Lt. Colonel Mammary F.

In lieu of flowers, please send donations to Dr. Plastic's office.

19

BALANCE

Who knows about being off balance better than a mono-boob? Having cancer has been a reminder of the importance of balance in my life. Balance between work and play, between love and distance, between self and other, between healthy and unhealthy. Every day presents with so many choices, from "Do I take a nap or spend time helping my son solve a crossword puzzle and watch *Dora the Explorer* with my little girl?" "Do I eat what I like or choose what is more nutritious?" "Do I think about the thirty percent of women who don't make it to five years after diagnosis or the seventy percent who will?" It's a constant balancing act.

Some days my biggest accomplishment is to flip through a *Victoria's Secret* catalog without crying. One of the down sides of having a mastectomy is the feeling of being excluded from something that you were part of for a long time. I used to circle the lingerie section at stores just to check out my options, but now I feel like I don't belong there. My options are now relegated to matronly specialty stores crowded by ladies my mother's age. They say chemo ages a person ten years and they're right. I sometimes feel like I'm living the life of a fifty-year-old. The hot flashes confirm the suspicion. I never anticipated having hot flashes at forty-one, but suddenly, a bunch of fifty-year-olds and I are chums because we can both bitch about night sweats.

Ever since my mastectomy, I feel lopsided, like I'm constantly taking a right turn. My run doesn't have the same rhythm. The plop-plop plop-plop is just plop...plop. Every time I look in the mirror, my chest winks at me. I do thank the surgeon for leaving a small part in the middle intact so could pull together a deceiving cleavage (if I ever dare to). Another advantage of having both breasts is that they hide the protuberant belly. Now with the breast gone, I get a better view of the steroid-enhanced roundness, and believe me, I don't want to see that. Steroids make me hungry, and after chemo there is only so much salad and cucumber a gal can eat before the cookie box beckons. It's not me, it's the steroids!

I remember when my son Shuja was born. I wanted to breast-feed him right away. What I didn't know was how newborns root for the nipple. I panicked, thought my baby was blind and couldn't see where to latch. Thankfully it was just new-mother fear. I breast-fed both my children for at least one year. Those are some of the wonderful memories of the mammaries, and the love and bond they created between me and my children cannot be understated. I feel the loss, and I think they do too. It's as if one of their favorite childhood comfort toys got broken. The great thing about children is their resilience. They don't obsess over stuff for too long. Not like adults. It's something we can all learn from the little ones in our homes.

I used to consider myself a bit of an artist until I had to draw eyebrows on my face. I have always appreciated nice eyebrows on others but never paid a lot of attention to my own. Fortunately, I didn't have the bushy ones or the unibrow or any other variant that requires regular grooming. They were light, nicely shaped, and just right.

Cut to chemotherapy and a faint line of abandoned stubborn hair hangs out on my supra-orbital ridge. Until now, I never realized the contrast eyebrows bring to a face. Being a regular on TV shopping channels, I always doubted make-up artist claims that "Brows frame the face." But they're right. So after much research online, I bought an eyebrow pencil. How hard could it be to draw two eyebrows? Obviously, I had no idea.

The key challenge of course is that they have to match. It's easy to fill gaps in an existing shape, but creating brows out of nothing is tough. Can you imagine a patient walking into their psychiatrist's office and finding that one of the doctor's eyebrows is perpetually raised? The brain automatically intuits this gesture as disapproval, creating all sorts of self-esteem issues in the patient. If I draw the brows too high, I look perpetually amused. If I draw them too low, I appear more depressed than the patient. Press the pencil too hard and I look ready for my juggling act.

Most folks with cancer rant about losing the hair on their heads (and I have too), but it turns out that losing those seemingly insignificant little nose hairs is the bigger deal. Yes, chemo makes those fall out too, which leads to an ongoing love affair with nasal saline spray. I'm constantly sniffling and cleaning my congested nose and dealing with a not-so-occasional nose bleed. Before cancer I didn't appreciate the functional aspect of my eyelashes. Turns out, they're there for a purpose (and not just to fund the billion dollar cosmetic industry). Nevertheless, you have to adapt, accept, and keep moving. These are minor inconveniences for the promise of a cancer-free life.

Worth it?

Totally!

An additional bonus is finding yourself and your strength along the way. Sometimes just hiding the weakness is strength. It's hard to stay focused on the goal when your body is protesting with fatigue and the end still seems far away. There are days of exhaustion, itchy palms, episodes of diarrhea, pain all over the body, aching bones and joints. You weave in and out of life; three days to rest and recover, three days to live, and then back to chemotherapy. Trying to keep the fabric of your life intact. Being hands-on with kids on good days and then letting it go for the days you can't. Zooming in and out of the window of your life, hoping to stay there for a while longer. All other goals are secondary. The first one is really the one that matters—to stay alive and fight because in a fight, your strength isn't measured by anything but the belief that you will win.

I will win.

THE END OF TREATMENT GONG

20

THE WAITING ROOM

Walking into a cancer clinic waiting room, you're hit with a wave of dreadful anticipation. A halo of worry, like a thick fog, looms over every individual sitting there. In many ways, all the faces look the same, tired and worn. There's a creepy homogeneity among patients. They sit staring at their palms or somewhere far, fantasizing a place devoid of illness and suffering while trying to stay afloat in the sea of apprehension. Smiles seem utterly out of place. Everyone is far too overwhelmed with personal angst to reciprocate social niceties.

No one wants to be here. No one wants to make eye contact. No one wants to occupy this disconnected group of chairs arranged symmetrically in a large carpeted room. The meaningless art on the walls is of no interest to those who are dealing with a life threatening illness. There is "healing garden" outside, but during a Midwestern winter, it looks ghastly.

I have been to plenty of other hospital waiting rooms. There's always a hum of chatter and the noise of TVs keeping those who await occupied. Labor and delivery waiting rooms are particularly lively as families learn about the new arrivals.

But here, in the cancer clinic waiting room, the hustle and

bustle is muted. It's as sterile as an OR, devoid of positive feelings and occupied by unwilling participants. Here the choices are "No evidence of disease" or "It's back." But no one ever dares to use the word "cure."

Even the coffee here is run down. The Styrofoam cup is flimsy and won't balance right because there is a little extra nubbin on the bottom that prevents complete contact with the table.

It has been two years since my diagnosis of breast cancer. Of course the further away you are from the diagnosis, the better. The two-year landmark is critical since ninety percent of recurrences seem to happen in the first two years. However, I am far from feeling that I have survived. My life in no way resembles what it was two years ago, and I am not the same person who arrived here for the first time, scared and anxious.

I do not look forward to these appointments. I never sleep well the night before. Even though today is just a "routine follow up" with no anticipated surprises, I have to admit that I'm nervous. I have been feeling well generally, except for the tiredness. Tired is my new normal. And the joint pain, yes of course, I need to tell her about the joint pain.

I look up to see if the nurse that just came out is looking for me, but she calls out an older gentleman who is slowly getting up from his chair. A younger woman is with him with a big tote bag, and I see knitting needles poking out. I can tell they are here for chemotherapy. Those who come for chemotherapy usually bring supplies to keep them occupied, so it looks like the father will get chemo, and she will work on her knitting project. I have spent enough time in this room to know how to decipher these relationships.

The day I was diagnosed, I walked into this waiting room with a heavy heart. I knew this place would be my hangout for many months in the near future. Being the doctor, the waiting room is the least familiar room for me in a hospital. I knew what ORs looked like, the setting of a delivery room, and where to find extra boxes of tissues, but this was new terrain. I was used to sitting inside the exam room on the spinning chair. I ran the show. I was not the one who sat in the waiting room nervously wondering. The tables had turned on me.

Doctors fight for life, but it is the patient's battle. Suddenly it was my turn to fight.

Every time I came to this waiting room, I worried about my life and my future. Is the chemotherapy even working? Is it going to be worth it? Will I survive this cancer, or will I be a statistic that haunts other survivors?

I would imagine the receptionists talking in hushed tones, "Remember her? The one who always smiled and cracked jokes? The doctor? Well, I heard she died last week." Then I would imagine them commiserating on how sad it was until another patient came to check in, getting their entry pass into the cancer world.

I would sit and look at other patients and try to guess what kind of cancer they had. What must their prognosis be? Are they here for a routine follow up, chemotherapy, or something else? Are they dying or are they living? Do they know yet?

Then I would wonder about myself. Am I dying or am I living? Will I die or will I live? Why am I even here? What purpose does my being alive serve?

The time during acute cancer treatment is daunting. I suddenly appreciated life like never before. I wanted to live every day; the problem is that it's so hard to enjoy life when the sword hangs over your head. There are no sure-shot answers when you deal with cancer. There are possibilities and probabilities. You don't want to think about it, but you want to prepare yourself to face death, should that be your destiny. You reassess your relationships and run the tape forward to see how they will function once you're gone.

The plants in this waiting room look fake, which is consistent with the theme of this place—the space between alive and dead. I fit somewhere in that scheme. Still alive, still not dead. That is the dilemma of a cancer survivor. The negotiation between these two extremes.

Do I reengage with life fully as I was?

Do I withdraw under the fear that it might end?

The one thing that having had cancer does is obliterate the imagined distance between life and death. Instead of two opposites, they become two parallel thoughts. They walk together holding hands throughout your life. You spend a lot of time figuring out which one you're closer to.

The waiting room of life and death. I sat here for the first time two years ago and I sit here today, a changed woman. I still fear death but I have seen it so closely that the fear has abated. The repeated exposure has attenuated the fear.

They only way to surpass the fear is to capture each moment and make it worthwhile. To be there when life is gracious in hours and years. To catch every second thrown at you.

Do I make out alive this time? I don't know yet. But this much I do know: I am not dead yet.

21

INVISIBLE SCARS

The feeling I most clearly remember is fear—an overwhelming wave of fear gripping my body. My breath coming out in gasps, wrestling against the suffocating force of a heavy weight on my chest. There was a churning feeling inside, a dark apprehension that something awful had occurred. I was slipping helplessly, down towards an unknown abyss. The speed and the horror were escalating. Suddenly I look down and, to my severe dismay, notice that my entire left breast is reduced to a pouch of blood, jostling as I slid. I wake up before I could scream.

Disoriented, I attempt to grasp my reality.

A quick peek into my nightgown reveals a large, jagged, healed-over mastectomy scar. With ambivalent joy I inhale deeply. My cancer-filled left breast is no longer attached to me. "It was two years ago. You are okay now." A few neurons reluctantly fire in my brain and I regain my sense of time.

In the past two years, I underwent a complete mastectomy, sixteen cycles of chemotherapy, and thirty-three sessions of radiation. After treatment, I was handed broken pieces of my life and told to go rebuild what I had lost. My mastectomy scar has certainly healed, but have I?

The journey to healing fully from breast cancer truly begins once all the treatments end. It is a long and tedious process, punctuated with unrelenting stress and anxiety that continues for years. It's a process that requires tremendous amount of coping, acceptance, and negotiation, followed by a lifetime of fear and anxiety.

Having breast cancer is a physically and psychologically intense trauma. The assault on femininity, the fear of death, the angst of the surgeries and reconstruction, infertility, baldness, relentless nausea during chemotherapy, chronic aches and pains, low energy, fatigue, and many other medical complications are just the tip of the iceberg.

Beginning at the time of diagnosis, it's a process of re-traumatization.

Ask any cancer survivor, the toughest phase of this journey is the time when newly diagnosed. The words "You have cancer" will shake anyone to the core. No matter how strong you thought you were before, the anxiety, fear, and helplessness of those first few days is insurmountable.

Despite being a trained psychiatrist, I wasn't immune to any of it.

Sleep was hard to come by without pills, and Xanax was my friend during the day. The knowledge and training about the human intra-psychic world did little to alleviate my panic. I started to look for answers to understand my emotional upheaval and realized that I had symptoms of Post Traumatic Stress Disorder.

PTSD is no longer considered solely the result of a war trauma. Turns out that severe trauma of any kind can cause these symptoms—and cancer is no exception. The available data indicates that one out of four breast cancer survivors experience PTSD. It's a staggering number of people going untreated and undiagnosed.

PTSD can manifest as symptoms of avoidance, re-experiencing (nightmares or daytime flashbacks), and hyperarousal. It can cause persistent anxiety, panic attacks, racing heart, and inability to relax or sleep. Most trauma victims will desperately avoid triggers or reminders of their trauma incident. But cancer survivors don't have the luxury of avoidance. They return over and over again to the hospital and the cancer clinic, peppered with constant reminders of their initial trauma. Each visit to the doctor can be triggering. The medical community is in denial of this aspect of the cancer process and remains poorly responsive to the emotional needs of survivors.

During my two years of treatment, only once did a social worker meet with me to assess if I was "doing okay." It was a brief visit while I was attached to the chemotherapy infusion, drowsy and tired. Her conclusion was that no further follow up was necessary.

My skills and training were useful in gathering support through this very difficult time, but I struggled with the idea of how unrecognized and unmet my emotional needs were. Feedback from other survivors indicated that this is a common occurrence. Only rarely were they referred to a support group or offered medication or therapy referrals.

Since patients tend to focus mostly on their physical symptoms, it is imperative for oncologists and breast surgeons to take the lead and ask routinely about the emotional status of their patients. In fact, a complete assessment of a survivor's emotional status at the time of diagnosis should occur. This needs to be reviewed at regular intervals during and at least two years out of treatment since data points to persisting symptoms.

Each newly-diagnosed person should get at least two appointments with a mental health professional to assess their level of acceptance and coping with the diagnosis. I have yet to meet a fellow survivor who has escaped emotionally unscathed from the cancer experience. The need is imminent and acute, but it is not being addressed.

In this day and age of ever shrinking funding to mental health services, no fundraising efforts are being made to address this unmet need of millions of survivors. Cure and awareness are the song of the month without attention to the emotional needs of those who actually do survive. Breast cancer survivors, if and when "cured," will still suffer from the consequences of this trauma.

Healing from cancer cannot occur without complete emotional healing.

Just a few weeks ago, I went back for my routine mammogram. I sat in the same waiting room for thirty long minutes, and when I inquired about the delay, the receptionist was rude. Before I knew it, tears were rolling down my cheeks. This was the exact waiting room where I once said good-bye to my cancer-free life and body.

I still carry those scars, the raw and the invisible ones.

22

WHAT I LEARNED

At this point, I am still figuring out the semantics of having cancer. Is it "I have cancer," "I have had cancer," or "I had cancer"? At what point do you become a survivor?

I bought a charm and some other items inscribed with the word survivor, but I'm not sure when I can wear them. I know I'm a fighter. I have always been. I am empowered, and will always be. But when do I have the privilege to say, "I have survived"? I have survived being told "You have cancer." I have survived a mastectomy and chemotherapy. I have endured.

Are you a survivor when you're done with treatments? Are you a survivor when the first post-treatment scan is clean? My personal conclusion is that surviving the words "You have cancer" earns you the status of survivor. You've handled that life-changing phone call, the ominous tone in the doctor's voice, the pause, the anxiety, the nervousness, and the hesitation. Then, once the news is out, you've handled the disbelief, the shock, the flashback of your entire life. Then the denial, "But I have a life to live! I have kids, I have a home, a husband, a career!" If you've survived all that, you're a survivor.

So I guess I've earned the right to wear my survivor paraphernalia. But now, the three words even scarier than "You have cancer" are "recurrence," "metastasis," and "hospice."

Perhaps being a survivor means being able to live past those scary thoughts. Past the fear of being told that at any time you may get the signal to pack up and go. Past the idea that you may not live to be old. I have to admit, I now fantasize about getting dementia because that would mean I lived a long life. By the way, the psychiatrist in me wants to clarify that there are indeed dementias that happen in early years, but I'm not rooting for those. I want the one that comes with being on this planet for eight or nine decades. Turning fully grey used to be a fantasy. Now thanks to chemo, the regrowth is all grey. How much life is enough anyways? Long enough for your children to grow old, get settled, have kids? At what point does one say, "I have lived long enough"?

Perhaps being a survivor means having had a chance to think about those questions and have your answer ready, being aware of the value of life. Perhaps being a survivor means living life mindfully, having survived the ignorance of spending days without thought, having survived the lack of appreciation of being healthy, having survived knowing what fighting for your life means.

I hope I am a mindful survivor. Ready to resume life. Ready to survive the next curveball while holding onto that other ball called "I had cancer."

I read a Buddhist saying: "The teacher appears when the student is ready." In the learning of life, I believe I was ready when the cancer arrived.

I am sure you've heard cancer survivors say that they've learned a lot through this journey. Some even go so far as to say they would do it all over again and not change a thing. I wouldn't say that—I would jump at the first opportunity to hear "You are cured" or even, "Sorry, it was all a big mistake." But if it has chosen me, I accept and embrace it.

I was reflecting on what I learned. To begin with, having cancer is like knowing how to ride a bicycle. It's something you never forget. Perhaps you have a few moments when it escapes your consciousness, but it always comes back. It's always there.

Being diagnosed with a life threatening illness carries many lessons, most of them deep and meaningful, but some are shallow and practical. For example, how to take off a winter hat without dislodging your wig, how to adjust your prosthesis in Target without anyone noticing, how to quickly fill in disappearing eyebrows, how to style and wash wigs, how to apply fake eyelashes, how to use spray on lotion. I have learned that life is as wonderful with one breast as with two, that mastectomy swimsuits are not all matronly, and that a newly shaved head itches a lot.

I have learned that kind words, spoken or written, have magical healing powers. I learned that when some people speak, they are merely exercising their glossal muscles and what comes out of their larynx should be ignored like the sound of working machinery. I have learned that a sugar buzz can fix melancholia on certain days (donuts for breakfast are a new discovery for me) and that beautiful fragrances can be uplifting even when food doesn't taste good. I always carried two bottles of essential oils, lemon and peppermint, in my chemo bag. The smell of fresh citrus is life reaffirming and helps with nausea. Every chemo morning I would wear a sweet, floral fragrance to perk me up. But because smells also evoke memory, I know that I will no longer use that perfume.

I have also learned that wearing a thick eyeliner hides missing eyelashes, that two strokes of blush makes a world of difference, and that without eyebrows and lashes, my eyes look reptilian. I have learned that a good nurse can make a world of difference and that people generally are inclined to help, if they can.

I have learned that true friends can fill your heart with joy and strangers can convey surprising warmth. I have learned that you don't need much in life—the key is to appreciate what you have. However, on certain days a little shopping spree doesn't hurt. I have learned that having a positive self-esteem is the best asset. But on days when you are unsure of your own strength, faith can fill in the blanks very effectively. I have learned that love attracts love, compassion attracts compassion, and that life has to be dealt with on a daily basis. If each day, I can say honestly to myself, "I did something useful," then the number of months or years doesn't matter. Making others happy is sometimes the only way to have a good day.

I have learned that one can live with fear. That it is possible to not give fear power over your life, to not give disappointment dominance over hope, and to look at the rainbow and deny the clouds. I've learned that it's possible to ignore pain in pretty much any body part, given the right state of mind, and that taking sleep medication isn't a personal failure. I have seen hope, in its most advanced and rudimentary forms, and I know that if there isn't a tomorrow, there is a later.

I have often wondered what the popular phrase "Kick cancer's butt" really means. I discovered that it means holding your head high and not being afraid of death; living every day with grace, dignity, and hope. It's a state of mind and a mode of behavior and has nothing to do with your physical experience or endurance. The fact is this: All cancer patients are getting mostly the same treatment and care.

I do think however that it would be quite therapeutic if the oncology clinic had a large bean bag labeled CANCER that patients could kick with all their might at the end of treatment. Wouldn't that be cool?

23

BREAST ENVY

As a psychiatrist, I am very familiar with the concept of penis envy as proposed by Sigmund Freud. But what I had never experienced until recently was breast envy. Yes, the envy of other women who have two breasts. My trip to a water park uncovered this psychological issue.

The first day upon arrival at the resort, I used my wig as an excuse to avoid the water. Chlorine will ruin it, I claimed. (I was equally unsure about whether my hand-drawn eyebrows might dissolve.) I had read that all prostheses absorb and expand in water, and I was nervous about this expanding proposition. So I spent most of the time curled in the lounge chair staring at other women and their breasts. I was like a kid watching other kids eat ice cream after a scoop of mine fell on the ground—envious and wistful, thinking, "I once had two of those, too."

Women walking around in swimsuits, women with two breasts, women without "ports" in their chests, women with hair, women with ponytails, women with eyebrows, women with eyelashes, women with toned abs. I watched a mammarily gifted woman in a cheetah-print swimsuit strut languidly by and mused, *How would she react if I walked up to her and complimented her breasts?*

Cancer gives you courage, but also the wisdom to not use said courage on all occasions. I kept the compliment to myself.

The toughest thing about the grief over the loss of a breast is that you never get the chance to mourn it fully before the whirlwind of treatment starts. When someone dies, there is usually a service, then the family gets a chance to gather and regroup, hopefully comforted by loved ones. When your breast dies, the postmortem report (i.e., the pathology report,) is handed to you, usually with more disturbing information than the demise itself. Then instead of a quiet period of mourning, you are sent off to deal with the harsh reality of chemotherapy. No break, no memorial, no time to grieve. So as you recover from chemo, you get moments here and there to work through the grief, and therefore, it isn't unusual for some to experience grief that lasts a lifetime.

Having had a few patchy moments of working through my grief, I felt ill-equipped to handle the breast-fest around me. I envied the women in their two-piece bikinis. Being a modest woman, I would never be caught dead in one, but just knowing I couldn't rock one like some of them bothered me. I could never buy a regular swimsuit anymore and will always have to get a mastectomy suit with a high neck. I had to keep reminding myself to take the prosthesis out of my swimsuit before throwing it in the water extractor. I couldn't get myself to use the shower in the women's locker room. I imagined being looked at and discussed in hushed tones by the teenagers with body piercings.

The next day, I decided I wanted to have fun, so I put my cap on (instead of the wig) and got in the water. It felt nice. The statistic of one in eight women in the U.S. having breast cancer was weirdly reassuring—chances are that I wasn't the only one afflicted in this huge water park. There must be others here, struggling just like me. I took the ride on the lazy river, the only thing I usually do at the water park. I am not for the slides. For one thing, I don't know how to swim, and secondly, I was always too scared. My kids, on the other hand, are little daredevils. My husband asked the kids if they wanted to go down the big slide in the family raft, and they jumped at the chance. Knowing that I don't do rides, he said to me, "You can stand over there and you will see us come out."

Suddenly, I heard myself asking, "Can I come too?"

He looked at me puzzled, "You mean on the ride?"

"Yes," I said simply and joined them in line.

Three times I came down the slide in the raft screaming at the top of my lungs, completely ignoring the sinking feeling I got as the raft plunged downhill, completely ignoring the fact that I can't swim. I embraced that moment of thrill, the here and now.

I am no longer afraid!

Cancer does that to you. And during the ride it didn't really matter if I had one breast or two.

Is my life the
act of knowing
who I am and where
I am? Is my life the
people around me?

Or is it my beating
heart and my
breathing lungs?

24

THE 24-HOUR COCKTAIL PARTY

I have been up since 3:00 a.m. I don't know what people did before smartphones when they woke up in the middle of the night. Now, the world is always wide awake next to you, and at 3:00 a.m., you can conveniently walk out of your bedroom and blend into the other half of the "awake" world. You seamlessly enter discussions and make comments without the awkwardness of "Why are you up at this hour?" The 24-hour cocktail party is on and it's easy to join the conversations of work slackers on the other side of the world and the perpetual insomniacs on this side.

I am not a perpetual insomniac. I like to sleep when I can. I know exactly what to take and how much to get enough sleep. Today, however, I am trying hard for this night not to turn into dawn. I know that during the early morning hours when you want to sleep but can't, when your mind has an eerie clarity about life despite your heavy eyelids, those early hours feel long. They feel long because they defy expectation. I would like to sleep but can't. That makes the minutes last longer and hours feel like forever. I want to extend this time. I don't want Monday to arrive.

Last night I was trying to figure out how to bottle my being into something permanent. A friend of mine has a birthday next weekend, and I was looking for a present for her. I know she likes my taste in gifts. Is there a way I can preserve that? Pass on my good taste and my knack for gift-giving to my kids? A slice of me.

What is the extent of my life? How wide does it spread? From one country to another where my loved ones are, or is it narrower? What is the reach of my life? Is it everyone I have met and touched? My virtual acquaintances? What precisely is the area my life occupies in this world? Is it the little chunks of caring in everyone's hearts that I have known, or is it just me within my body?

Does my life actually reside within my children who have my genes? How big or small is my life? One human among a sea of billions on the revolving Earth.

Is it as small as a frame of five-foot-four and 130 pounds or as big as a particle of energy that belongs to the whole universe? Does the size of my life matter? Does the size of those few millimeter lesions that were seen on my liver on Saturday matter? Just a cluster of a few cells. My entire body is nothing but cells.

But it feels like life is shrinking longitudinally and simultaneously expanding to the horizons of concerns and fears, of hope and faith. What are the boundaries of my psychological life? The waves of fear and anxiety, moments of laughter, times of self reflection, of joy, of pain.

Is my life the act of knowing who I am and where I am? Is my life the people around me? Or is it my beating heart and my breathing lungs?

We so casually use the phrase, "This is my life." But exactly how much life does this word "life" contain, and what are the limits?

My life in years, my life in breaths, my life in love, my life in objects, the books that line the cases, earrings neatly arranged in a box, clothes hanging in the closet. Where is me and how much is me?

Is my life mine? "My" is a word of full ownership and control. "Mine" is a word of security and a commitment. But was it ever mine?

Life—a mosaic of moments, things, genes, scenes, emotions braided through the fabric of our universe and I am a spot somewhere.

The spot that shines—with breaths and beats—and that dulls down eventually.

My life, a spot, a juncture, a happening, a few moments of alignment of the components of life. Then those components come undone only to blend together for another spot to shine.

I am up thinking about my life because I don't want Monday to arrive. Monday will reveal the nature of the spots in my liver. A few more ingredients thrown into the mix to make metastatic cancer.

The scanner is ready to be part of my story again.

Is my life my liver? It's the part of me that decides whether I dull or whether I shine?

Is cancer my life or merely a part of me? Where does it start and where does it end? Cancer, the unmanaged growth ready to shrink my life.

It's woven together: me, life, and cancer. Something grows, something shines, and something dulls.

I want you to leave
so my friends can rejoice
and my family can breathe.
I need you to leave so that my
patients can rest assured that
the one person who truly
understands them is still
there and they won't have
to start over with
a stranger.

25

LETTER TO CANCER

Dear Cancer,

Believe me, you aren't dear to me; I'm merely sticking to epistolary convention. You have enjoyed the stay in my body for much too long and have overstayed your welcome. I would like you to pack your stuff and leave. My body has better things to do than to fight with your megalomania. There is an exit sign that you are ignoring.

There is a lot this body still needs to accomplish and you have lodged yourself in a space reserved for someone else. I need the room vacated so it can be filled with joy and peace and contentment.

I need my energy so that I can see my children grow. My son needs you to leave so he can grow up to be a man but still have a place where his tears are not seen as weakness. My daughter needs you to leave so she can be all that she needs to be.

I need you to leave so I can grow old with my loving husband. He needs you to leave so he can have his life back, so he doesn't have to be mother and father. He needs you to leave so he can lose the anxiety of losing the love of his life.

You have been trying to suck the energy out of me for far too long—bit by bit, piece by piece. You don't scare me, and I can look your sick mitotic nuclei in the eye and say, "I am not afraid." But my family is scared and so I just need to you to leave.

I want you to leave so my friends can rejoice and my family can breathe. I need you to leave so that my patients can rest assured that the one person who truly understands them is still there and they won't have to start over with a stranger.

I want you to leave so I can look at those who abandoned me during cancer and say, "Thank you for helping me realize that you never mattered. I won this battle without you!"

I need you to leave because I have learned all the lessons that I needed to learn from looking death in the eye. I have learned not to take anything, or anyone, for granted. I have learned to take each moment as it comes. To find meaning and hope in every day life. To make things happen and not wait. To be myself and trust myself. To be honest and forthright. To endure.

I have learned the meaning of pain and suffering. I now know that a peaceful night's sleep is a blessing, being able to digest food is a treat, to be pain-free is a miracle, to feel energetic is a gift.

I am ready to move on from the lessons I have learned so I would like you to move on, too. Leave me alone. And at my next chemo appointment, when the Taxol infusion is flowing through my blood, I would like it to find you and tell you so.

It's time for you to move on. It's time for me to start over.

Yours (not if I can help it!),

A Cancer Survivor

26

CAN I QUIT CHEMO?

- Can I quit chemo so I don't have to feel the needle entering my port?
- Can I quit chemo so I don't spend two hours of my shortened life in the waiting room?
- Can I quit chemo so I don't have to sit with a group of unlucky souls each getting drenched in cytotoxicity?
- Can I quit chemo so I can gain a day to enjoy with my family?
- Can I quit chemo so I don't go in feeling well and come out feeling worse?
- Can I quit chemo so I can have hair and complain about bad hair days?
- Can I quit chemo so I don't need to draw eye brows or hide my chameleon eyes?
- Can I quit chemo so I don't vomit my guts out or roll in pain when my tummy hurts?
- Can I quit chemo so I can feel again what being rested feels like?
- Can I quit chemo so I can keep walking on my two feet?
- Can I quit chemo so I don't wait for scans and results?

- Can I quit chemo because my body is slowly crumbling from these chemicals?

- Can I quit chemo so I can be me again?

- Can I quit chemo so I can live again, even if it's for a short time?

But no, I can't. I am a warrior of hope, a cancer soldier. And one day, they will sit in a circle and say to each other: "She fought till the last minute. She didn't quit." Did I?

27

MRI

There are three letters of the alphabet that, when put together, make me uncomfortable: MRI.

A fear of MRIs suggests a pathetic state of affairs for it indicates surveillance, strict medical surveillance. Waiting for the body to do something forbidden, something illegal.

I had my fourth MRI today. The reason for this exam is "post-chemo leg weirdness" and it has been decided that an MRI of the knee may rule out anything serious. Not sure why, since breast cancer, if it metastasizes to the bone, will be better seen on a bone scan and not on an MRI which sees soft tissue better. But having the C-word attached to your medical chart earns you a lifetime of investigations, every new sensation yielding a "Why don't we..." and "Let's make sure..." and "It won't hurt to..." type of response from doctors.

After you've had cancer, your body can't be fully trusted. It's a body that has a mind of its own and could very well be quietly mounting a mutiny from within. No amount of investigations can restore this trust. This is true for trust in general. Once broken, we are left with a lifetime of apprehension and unnecessary hesitation. In the case of cancer, the betrayal is combated by vigilance.

"Lets make sure" it's just arthritis in your knee. "Why don't we" do a vascular ultrasound to make sure there aren't any clots. While we're in there, "it wouldn't hurt" to do a non-vascular ultrasound also.

None of the above tests were able to determine why my leg hurt. After reporting a normal knee, the radiologist throws in an MRI to confirm or rule out further causes. And there are those three letters: MRI.

I have always wondered if people who grow up in religious traditions that don't involve the grave fare better on MRIs. In my case, the MRI inevitably makes me feel like I'm being laid in a casket. Lying down is an extremely vulnerable position, in a narrow tight space even more so, needing to be very still, excruciating.

I hate MRIs. In my whole first year of cancer treatments, the only time I broke down and cried in the hospital was after my first breast MRI. Lying face down in a scanner with the breasts hanging through two openings in the table and then sliding into the scanner in a cold room alone, still freshly traumatized from my diagnosis, it was more than I could handle. I knew I needed to do it but how? Here I am, alone, without any distractions, just me and my thoughts. In a tube.

They always ask you before starting an MRI if you are claustrophobic. I don't think you can know whether or not you're claustrophobic until you have actually been inside an MRI scanner. Prior to my first scan, I had been in elevators and small rooms and closets without incident. But lying down in a tube is whole different story. I couldn't breathe. I gasped and I sighed and then tears started to roll down my cheeks. I tried hard not to move, although I felt like crying, crying in a way that set my whole existence in motion, but I couldn't.

The liver MRI happened under the most stressful circumstances. The day before I had been told, "The CT showed a spot on the liver. You need an MRI." That day I was broken from the inside. Death appeared more real than ever. The words "Stage IV" danced in my head. The technician doing the scan was a cheerful middle aged man who would periodically shout through the mic, "Breathe, breathe and hold." I tried hard to breathe. Holding my breath, I would wonder, what it was like to be dead? Do you even know that you're dead or in a grave? Do you see the zipper of the body bag being closed over you? Being still is depressing; it's one step away from being dead. Being human is the ability to walk and move and make noises and make funny faces. Lying still in a closed space is asking too much from an undead person. A person who wants to live, move, run. MRIs are not natural; they just aren't human.

So today, as the table gradually moved into the scanner, and the technician said, "I'm leaving," I panicked. A floodgate of emotions seemed to be approaching, much like the cold off-white surface of the scanner, and all of my body went into a narrow tube. It felt like I would never leave this thing, that it would close in on me and grab me hungrily to keep it company. My brain told me I was safe but the tightness of the space fought that thought and rendered it completely impotent.

I pressed the control for the technician to come back. She was kind and understanding. She recommended I close my eyes when I move inside the scanner. She made some conversation to put me at ease and then asked if we could start again.

The table started to move into the scanner. With my eyes tightly closed, I could still hear the tapping sound of the machine, but I was forcing my mind to imagine something else, anything else. Nothing was working. I started to pray. It helped for a while, but then the machine started to make deafening sounds. I knew it was just the magnet working, but that knowledge was useless. Think happy images! I managed to summon the image of my daughter making up a dramatic story about losing her tooth even though she is too young to. I pictured my son smiling as the sound of the knocking and hammering intensified.

I then started to attach visions to the sounds. I imagined a big Russian man with a loud voice saying "Da, da, da" as the machine made similar noises. Then I imagined another man who could say

"Tha, tha, tha" in a language that word might belong to. I imagined them fighting each other, the brawl getting louder and louder. The MRI machine goes in bursts. Once it starts to scan, there are periods of about five minutes when you have to lie still and bear the excruciating sounds.

I imagined being seated in the tail of an airplane where you can hear the engine roar. I imagined an embroidery machine with its needle swiftly moving back and forth. I finally started to time how long the Russian guy yells and how long the needle zigs and zags.

It's amazing how much a person can think about in 30 minutes. It can be a journey from life to death and back to life. A state of lying still, alone, unhindered, shallow breaths, gasps, and sighs. Aware of breathing at times but unsure if the air is actually going through the lungs. Maybe the air doesn't circulate in the scanner? Or does it?

The stillness of the whole room is penetrated by outside air as the technician walks in to confirm it's over. I get up and exhale, enjoying being able to sit up in an open space. My breathing still shallow, uncertain, just like the future after cancer.

PAINTING BY SAIRA MALIK REHMAN

28

2016 WAS...

2016 was the year I was supposed to go back to work full time.

2016 was the year I was diagnosed with metastatic breast cancer.

2016 was the year my daughter turned five, my youngest child. I had a princess party for her to celebrate that the worst was over. I had lived two years into my diagnosis. With ninety percent of recurrences happening in the first two years after treatment, I was so close to being out o the danger zone. I had ended all my active treatment in April 2014. So April 2016 did not seem to far away. The check-ups were steady and my oncologist had moved my appointments from every three months to every four months. I rejoiced. A threat that had arrived to ruin my life was just that, a threat. Emotionally, I was working hard to lessen the impact of that threat. I had begun writing about breast cancer and was active on social media educating others. I was working on accepting cancer as "a bump" in the road.

I was actively accepting new patients into my practice and looking forward to working more. I had even started some conversations about exactly what I wanted my career to look like now. I was looking forward to earning more too. I had always been quite financially independent and my income had taken a hit once I went part-time. The idea of earning significantly less than my husband was a tough pill to swallow. My fear of recurrence had started to decline. At my last appointment the doctor said I was "Looking the best I had in months."

Everything seemed liked it had started to fall back in its place somewhat.

Through all the gloom of cancer, hope had started to trickle that maybe I made it back with some semblance of what my life used to be. Spring was coming, and this year for sure I was going to plant more flowers.

I had been working out with a trainer at the gym to regain my strength, even though they assigned me the trainer who routinely worked with seniors. Nonetheless, I was kicking butt. I had almost lost all the weight that I had gained during chemotherapy. I had accepted Tamoxifen and was working with my doctor to transition to the aromatase inhibitors. I had accepted that I would be on medications for another seven years.

My "mathletic" kid would always say, "Mommy, I will be leaving for college when you get off these meds," and I would smile, hoping that I would be there to drive him to college. I would imagine what he would look like as a young man. His facial features, his hair, and his lanky frame. When he was born, the doctor said to me, "He will be a tall kid." I don't know how he knew that, but he had been delivering babies for 25 years and I was in no position to doubt such experience.

Then 2016 happened.

29

GOOD NIGHT, SON

I lay here next to him in his bed. His hair smells fresh and he is telling me something that happened at school today. I am trying to focus on the contents of his story, but my mind is drifting in and out.

It has been barely three days since my diagnosis of Stage IV metastatic cancer was confirmed. My nine-year-old boy lies next to me in his bed and I stare at the fan in his room. He gets hot easily and loves to have the fan running on high at night. The chain controls have two planets hanging from them. I am sure he can tell me which planets they are, along with their special features. They are spinning fast with the air, much like the thoughts in my head.

I am going in to meet the oncologist tomorrow. Tomorrow, my treatment plan will be determined. I am really hoping I get to keep my hair this time, not because that is the most important thing to me, but a hairless mommy is just a bit freaky to the kids. Nothing says cancer more than a bald head. I haven't told him yet.

He has grown up under the shadow of cancer for the last two and half years. He has seen me sick and he has seen me bald. I haven't been able to gather up the courage to tell him that my cancer has returned. I really don't know how to explain to him that his mother was diagnosed with an incurable illness. How do I destroy his innocence myself?

How do you explain to an nine-year-old the concept of death and loss?

I wish I had let him have a pet. A fish, a hamster, something small. Something small that had died. So I could tell how he handles grief. Something insignificant in his universe that could help me answer some of my questions. The Earth rotates and the planets spin. The glow-in-the-dark planet set hangs from the curtain rod as well. Everything in nature is supposed to stay in its place to keep the balance. But what about me and him? Why must I change his orbit?

My gaze catches the telescope that sits on the chest of drawers consistent with the theme of the room. He has been obsessed with planets and the universe since he was three. An early reader, he would bring these little planet books from the library, and we would read those to him over and over again. Later, and for the longest time, his favorite book was *Atlas of the Universe*. I would get inundated with universe factoids.

His universe is under threat by something that was seen under a microscope. Those metastatic cells, gang banging through my body, found a new home in my liver. He could tell that something was wrong when I had my liver biopsy. The next day when he came home from school, I was still in my pajamas, a very rare sight. That evening, he commented to his Dad, "Mommy looks just like she used to look when she had cancer."

My heart sank and a psychiatrist who always knows what to say was speechless. I made lame excuses and lied through my teeth.

The fan whirs and my mind continues to spin. How exactly do I sit down with him and what words should I use?

Twenty years of medical practice, discussing terminal diagnoses with patients, and one would think I'd have the skills to break this news to my son, but no! All this mother is capable of is wiping her tears and hiding her face in his comforter.

He says to me, "Mommy I think I've figured out what 'www'

means. I think it's the 'whole wide world' or something."

I wipe my tears and say, "Very close, it's the world wide web."

He cuddles with me some more; the whole wide world shrinks in my arms, and he dozes off.

The clock keeps ticking. It's the shape of an iPad. His chess trophies stare at me and the Legos stay still. He gently breathes in his sleep.

I think, *Thank God he has a telescope so he can watch Mommy when she becomes a star.* My eyes fill up again.

On the wall there's a Dr. Seuss decal that I thought would be good for him to look at every day: "Today you are You, that is truer than true. There is no one alive who is Youer than You."

Let him sleep one more night with his innocence. There is a lifetime ahead of him to learn about death and dying. I am alive today and that is truer than true.

Good night twinkling stars.

Good night heavenly bodies.

Good night, my Son.

Motherhood is a treacherous emotional journey, an experience that teaches you more than you ever wanted to know.

There is nothing comparable to the emotional growth it offers when you put a little person above and beyond all your needs.

30

MOTHER'S DAY

I want to skip Mother's Day this year. Do you know of a country that doesn't make a big deal about Mother's Day? Can I just quietly slide there without anyone noticing?

Can I please ignore all the preppy "Mommy and toddler rolling in the grass"-type TV ads? Can I pretend not to see the magazine pages of young moms aging to wise old moms? Can someone delete all emails I get about "You still have time" (mostly referring to buying stuff for Mother's Day)?

I would really like to not be reminded of Mother's Day this year.

I feel awful. I'm angry at myself. I feel guilty. I feel sad.

I'm a mom and I have metastatic breast cancer, the kind that kills.

Being a mother, "technically" (my son's favorite word) I should gladly participate in the annual honoring of moms. I should look forward to the printed pink gift bag packed with some combination of pretty mug, fragrant candle, fun print pajamas, spa certificates, or sparkly jewelry. I should be excited at the thought of receiving handmade cards. I should rejoice at the flowers and the chocolate-coated strawberries that I will duly "share" with my kids. (Read: get only one as they inhale the whole box.)

But I feel disengaged from all of it. I am just not feeling it this year. I feel like a lame-ass mother. I have never neglected my kids, or been an addict (Facebook addiction is questionable), or abused them (feeding them avocados and broccoli is NOT abuse), but the mother inside of me is ambivalent and distraught.

My motherhood is plagued with cancer. Those who know me will probably vow to my brilliance as a mother (okay, brilliance is somewhat of an exaggeration.) I think I can even get my kids to admit that I'm a good mom (coercion is a supermom skill), but in my heart I feel guilty and undeserving of this acknowledgment.

I do not want the tray of breakfast in bed. After post-chemotherapy spells of vomiting, can I please take a raincheck on anything to do with food (cooked or partially digested)?

One of my favorite rituals of Mother's Days past has been the traditional Pakistani breakfast served at Devon Avenue in Chicago. Last year, however, I couldn't tolerate the deep fried poori bread (more oil than in the Gulf States). I had adapted a low carbohydrate lifestyle after my diagnosis. (This does not mean that I don't eat fruits and vegetables, so you can stop right there with your dietary advice.) I was very nauseated after barely eating a quarter of it, and honestly, nausea does not trigger pretty memories.

As I was wiping my greasy fingers, I told myself, *The farther I move away from cancer, the more some of these awful memories will fade*. But that hope was taken away from me for good.

The cancer was back to reclaim the strength, hope, and courage it had mistakenly left behind. I am still trying to find a way to live peacefully knowing that my illness can no longer be cured. This mom now officially has incurable cancer.

For the last nine years, I have felt infinitely special to be a mom. I have understood the hard work, the pain, the sorrow, the joy, and the laughter parenting entails. My two children are the joy of my life—a life that now has been changed irreversibly. I may be that mom who took off before getting her job done. (Granted, a mom's job is never done.)

I have tried very hard to be the best mom I could be and do whatever it takes to raise my kids well. Medicine has been my first love, the one for which I left my country, the one for which I turned down what many would consider "good proposals" (I come from a culture of arranged marriages), the one for which I made many sacrifices. But when my son was born, I had no qualms about going part-time. I decided to remain part-time until my daughter turned five. A month after she turned five, the cancer returned as metastasis in the liver.

But such is life: When does anything ever work out as planned?

A month after the recurrence, I quit my practice completely so I could enjoy the upcoming summer with my family. I knew it was the right decision, at least for the time being, but I grieve the loss of my identity as a practicing physician for the past two decades. I worked through my entire treatment last time, through chemotherapy and through radiation, but this time the stakes are different. I want to maximize my time with my children.

Most often people don't fear death itself; it's the suffering that is scariest. When a mother suffers, a family suffers. I feel guilty for the suffering that all of us may be destined for. But I don't know how to protect them. The very basic job of a mother is to shelter her young ones from suffering. How do I customize my motherhood correctly?

As a psychiatrist, I know there is no one right way of loving a child as long as they subjectively feel loved. I understand deeply how important mothering is for building the self-esteem of a child. I am their mirroring object, their moral support, their nurturing influence, and their safe place.

Motherhood, as much as the joy it brings, has also started to haunt me, for I feel I am failing my children.

Two months ago, an MRI found spots on my liver—spots that come with an expiration date, a warning sign similar to when you attend a company meeting and are told about the declining profit margins with vague references to possible layoffs. That kind of feeling, when you know it's time to clean up your resumé and re-activate your LinkedIn account. The sinking feeling you get when you hear rumors that your employer may merge with a competitor, and nothing is guaranteed. This is when you do the math to see how many months you can make your house payments without a paycheck. I am having those dark feelings about motherhood. I may lose this job because cancer may get me laid off.

How do you smile at your "boss" when the resignation letter is sitting in your drawer?

Can I honestly promise my kids that I will keep their handmade cards forever? Or the little plant that my daughter will bring home from school? When I vow to water it every day, even on days when I feel awful, am I lying to her?

I think about the day my oncologist called to confirm that the spots on the MRI were indeed breast cancer that had spread to the liver. It was dinnertime. I quietly took the phone call and went back to serving dinner. My husband and I put the kids to bed following our nightly ritual. I had decided to wait to fall apart until after they went to bed.

I ruminate and battle these thoughts. I reflect on the essence of motherhood. I look at other moms with their pretty smiles and worries that don't extend beyond "What's for dinner?" or "What summer camp should I sign them up for?" with envy. I was one of them three years ago. I wish I hadn't been so stressed then about the things that seem so trivial now.

I also know that all mothers, with or without cancer, have at one point or another seriously doubted their skill as a parent. Every one of us has had a moment when we've gone off into a corner and muttered under our breath, "If only I had not birthed you!" in anger. Or the moment when we lost it and then felt guilty going to work.

Motherhood is a treacherous emotional journey, an experience that teaches you more than you ever wanted to know. There is nothing comparable to the emotional growth it offers when you put a little person above and beyond all your needs. Every mother can relate to the times she has held her pee, to the point of her bladder nearly bursting, only to fix lunch for her hungry child. Or the time when she woke up at 3:00 a.m. to check her child's fever. I have experienced many such moments and feel lucky for those times.

Motherhood is love and sacrifice and that is what I must deliver, with or without cancer. My motherhood has been the fire in my belly. I have fought hard to live for my kids.

So, perhaps, a celebration is in order this Mother's Day, with a hearty side of denial and hope.

And as far as next year…well, as my friends say, it isn't guaranteed for anyone.

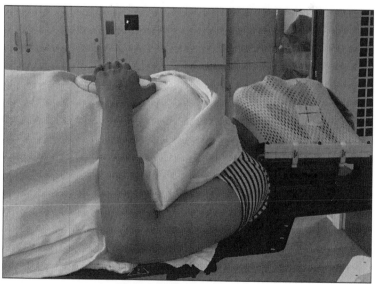

MASK FOR SKULL RADIATION

Since my recurrence,
I've often wondered if
I scared other survivors;
if seeing me reactivated
their own fears
of mortality.

31

I'M SORRY

Sorry, my apologies. With a diagnosis of metastasis four months ago, I didn't beat cancer.

Everyone said, "You're going to beat it." "If anyone can, you can!" They cheered me on as I endured one treatment after another, and I kept fighting "like a girl." I was told "You will kick cancer's ass and show cancer who is boss!" I rode the wave of positivity and determination. I believed it, too. I thrived on the fantasy of the cancer submitting to my will and strength.

Songs, inspirational quotes, memes, greeting cards and stories, all led to me to the one end point. Being a Type A personality, I accepted the challenge. I said to myself, I will beat cancer. Except for one open book exam, I have never failed at anything in life. So why not conquer this?

After the cancer metastasized, I felt like a failure, as if I let down everyone who thought I would "kick the shit out of cancer." I was no longer the example of how Stage III can be a success story and an inspiration. As a doctor, I understood that there was nothing I did to bring back my cancer. But I still felt a sense of shame.

Statistics indicate that thirty percent of those who are diagnosed with early stage cancer will develop metastasis, yet I had held onto the seventy percent dearly. Medical science currently doesn't know the exact mechanism through which cancer cells find a home in other organs of the body.

The time had come to let go of being a survivor and accept being a thriver or a lifer, the terms preferred by the metastatic community, since we ultimately end up not surviving the disease.

When I was diagnosed the first time, one of the things that helped me through treatment was supporting others with the same condition. I did this so their journey could be easier and smoother from my knowledge and personal experience. I wrote essays and participated in online groups.

Since my recurrence, I've often wondered if I scared other survivors; if seeing me reactivated their own fears of mortality. Sometimes I wondered if they actively avoided me. I am the face of incurable metastatic cancer, everything that anyone diagnosed with breast cancer is worried about. This is a real fear: this illness is terminal. It has no cure. I have no cure.

Having metastatic illness is an emotionally isolating experience. Many women I know tend to withdraw from others after metastasis because it's hard for others to understand our subjective experience, the experience of living life with an incurable, relentless illness with never-ending treatments. The concept is overwhelming.

I remember when I was first diagnosed in 2013, the word "metastasis" used to send chills up my spine. I used to dread #metsmonday showing up on my Facebook feed every Monday. I did not want to be reminded that my cancer could metastasize, although at Stage III with high-grade cancer cells, I knew inside that the odds of it happening were high.

One of my Stage IV friends has lived on with bone metastasis for eleven years. She gave me hope, but at times I would still try and block her out of my mind, for my own sanity, so I could worry less about me. That sounds selfish but the fear of recurrence is haunting.

I badly wanted to deny that it could happen to me. I convinced myself I was doing everything possible to reduce the chances of my recurrence. From good diet, exercise, supplements, and yoga, to lowering stress and getting enough sleep, and of course, all the medications and the treatments. I did everything possible to lower the chances of cancer taking root within me again.

But as time went on, I also worked hard on accepting what having had cancer means. It means accepting that your life will yo-yo between sweet fantasies and harsh realities. I got used to those ups and downs. I saw my friends with Stage IV cancers beat cancer on a daily basis. My denial softened gradually and I thought, *If metastasis happens, I will be okay.* I celebrated every clean scan and every good oncologist visit, but the fear of metastasis lingered.

And then it happened. I got another "I am so sorry" call from my doctor and I was devastated. Besides coping with my illness, I was sad that I lost my credibility as a cancer warrior who had "beaten" cancer. I was not longer a success story.

During all of this angst, I received this message from a fellow survivor whom I got to know via Facebook.

She wrote, "Until I 'met' you, I could not think of Stage IV. I'd panic, hyperventilate. Then I met you. You are showing me, with grace, passion and humor how this can be done. You are something of a role model to me. Doing this Stage IV before I do, if I do. I'm not so afraid anymore. I have someone doing this ahead of me and I know how to do it. If I ever get metastasis, I will have someone to emulate...and I will think of you the whole time. Forgive me if this bugs you. I just admire you so much and thank God for putting you in my life, but I am also so very, very sorry for your cancer."

And then I realized: I really don't need to "beat cancer." I have to beat life at its game, one day at a time.

Your manner indicates
you consider me a chart,
a number, a diagnosis,
yet another one at the
cancer center. But I am
a whole universe for
me and those who
love me.

32

LETTER TO ONCOLOGY CLINIC TRAINEE

Hi,

It's me, the patient you saw thirty minutes ago. I wanted to give you this feedback in person, but listening is not your strong suit, so I chose to write this.

Having been a physician now for over twenty years, I can usually tell by the way a student greets me whether a conversation will be worthwhile or not. Whether it's my personality, my power of observation, or the years of teaching others how to interview patients and engage them, but somewhere in that amalgam of knowledge, I have the ability to sense what a student truly seeks and how much of his or her attention is in the room with me.

There I was sitting on the exam table for the umpteenth time, drenched in the misery of metastatic breast cancer and the confines of its incurable boundaries, when you barreled in.

When a student walks into my exam room and calls me "Ms. Yunus," it tells me that she did not read my chart. You did try to pronounce my foreign name right, and I give you credit for that, but you addressed me in a way very few people have addressed me in my lifetime. I tolerate "Ms." instead of "Dr." just fine, unless it's paired with a bizarre sense of familiarity and an extra dose of feigned friendliness. I could tell the appointment would be interesting.

Your smile could have worked like sunshine, but it was more of an unwanted glare in my eyes. Artificially summoned cheer and familiarity is toxic in an oncology clinic. It's more suited, perhaps, at the beauty counter of a department store where something concrete can be offered up and accepted. An oncology clinic must dispense amorphous things, like hope and care, and it must do so with actual interest in (and humility for) the patient.

I could sense your quest to elicit all of my symptoms and cover your entire checklist. Just a gentle reminder for you and anyone in healthcare: Be genuinely interested and the diagnosis unfolds in front of you. There is no magic like empathy in medicine.

If a patient feels connected, she will take your hand and lead you to the most intimate places in her story, but to do that, you must unload your sense of authority and step inside. The two of you must belong in the same world for the length of the appointment. A healthcare provider cannot simply stand at the door, between sickness and health. No, she (or he) must transcend into the world of heartbreak and disability to get to know the patient.

Has anyone explained to you that a patient's exam room or a hospital room is a sacred space? Someone who is ill has lifted all of the curtains and opened all of the doors to let you in. The least you can do is not run her over with speed and callousness. Your breeziness and lack of good eye contact telegraphed you had an agenda.

Clearly, when a doctor and patient are in a room, there are two agendas at play. A successful appointment is the harmony of those two. I was hit on the head by your agenda to get every piece of information you needed, which put me off so much, I never gave you any information. That much control I have and I felt compelled to exert it.

As a cancer patient, I have seen my share of students—medical, physical therapy, CNA and nursing, and it's rare for me to be annoyed. After all, I remember my training days too: It was the graciousness of others who allowed me to examine them or draw their blood or share their story that made me the doctor I am today. I am forever grateful to have had the privilege to be a part of their story.

This is what I want you to learn.

Today, you have the white coat on and I am in the gown, yet you should know that it is I, the patient, who is giving you this opportunity to learn. So when you sit on your spinning stool, and shake your dangly earrings, be mindful that you have just entered my space and my life. I am vulnerable. My clothes are folded on a chair and I sit in a flimsy gown that barely covers my scarred body. I have lost control of my life to cancer and the fact that you are trying to exert authority over me, merely aligns you with my cancer instead of with me, the patient.

Your manner indicates you consider me a chart, a number, a diagnosis, yet another one at the cancer center. But I am a whole universe for me and those who love me. You ran through your checklist with a wink and a clicking tongue as you took a factory approach to healthcare. I was one more on the conveyor belt passing through. You may have learned that my organ systems are working in synchrony, but you didn't get to know me.

Do you realize why you were sent in to see me? It was not to wag your thick long ponytail as you asked me if my Minoxidil was working, and before I could answer, you filled in the silence with "Not so much?" Neither was it to have a "look and a listen"—your condescending terms for an adequate exam. You were sent into my space to help and heal me. That is what a patient comes into the clinic expecting.

Did you realize I told you nothing? Absolutely nothing?

After cancer, I deeply understand who is—and isn't—worth my time.

I bet you were surprised when the attending came, and I started talking and telling him all of the things I chose not to tell you.

As a side note: If you want to examine someone's armpit for lymph nodes, please make sure you stand right in front of the patient and she rests her hand on your shoulder, relaxing the surrounding muscles so you can access the nodes high up in the axilla. If you make the patient lift her arms like a bat, you're likely to miss nodes.

It's okay to let your patient realize you are still learning. Nothing connects more with a patient than a vulnerable medical professional. It's okay to say you don't know, or you will find out, rather than "Oh, yeah, that happens!" with a wink and a snappy tongue click.

Empathize when a patient tells you they are in pain and say you are sorry they suffer. An all-knowing smile and a head shake with an unrelated follow-up question simply play with the pain.

Yes, I am a patient, and today I denied you the privilege to be part of my intimate story. I wish you luck in your training and hopefully what you did was all a result of grave inexperience.

I wish I could have told you all this in person. I would have, if I believed you came to listen.

Sincerely,

Dr. Uzma Yunus

33

CLEANING OUT THE CLOSET

Today I decided to purge my closet.

Cleaning out the closet is hard. Memories are everywhere:
The shirt I wore after my daughter was born, the top I wore
on my son's first birthday, the khaki I loved wearing to work in the
summertime, business suits reminding me of job interviews, and the
power I felt in them—all reminders of what I have lost. My grief
hangs in hangers all around me. I embolden myself to let go. Ah,
yes, the big cancer lesson: Let shit go. Especially anything that has
no relevance to the life I live now and stirs up feelings of resentment.

There is that low-cut shirt I loved; the neckline always
challenged my modesty. It is the one shirt that reminds me of the
cleavage I once had and spent years hiding with camisoles and tanks.
It reminds me of my femininity and I wonder if I still possess it.

With a heavy heart, I make the decision that all pre-cancer
clothes need to go. It is just too hard to go through them over and
over again. The pants that don't fit, the top I wore to my CBS interview, the favorite sweater that worked as a default jacket on warmer
days, and my entire Ann Taylor work collection.

After I had my first child, I was committed to losing weight
because I felt I had hundreds of dollars invested in my wardrobe.

Now, my pudgy menopausal belly haunts me and none of the clothes fit.

I'm cleaning out all the clothes that I wore as an ordinary woman—before I became this "inspirational" character. That certainly wasn't my intention. In fact, sharing my breast cancer story publicly was a challenge. I was raised in a culture of inhibition, in which women aren't allowed to engage in such public discourse, especially when it comes to their female anatomy. In Pakistan, there is still a huge stigma associated with cancer. Once diagnosed, most assume it to be a death sentence—and who can blame them when treatment facilities are so few and far between.

Before I decided to "come out" with my story, I kept wondering if sharing all the details would affect my job prospects in the future. Discrimination in the workplace isn't relegated to race, sex, age, or gender. I had heard stories of cancer survivors losing out on positions because of their health history.

Nonetheless, I felt the urge to make my experience public for the sake of thousands of women (and men) who don't have the ability or the luxury to do so. I needed to speak up and tell the whole world the story of what it truly means to be a breast cancer survivor. I wanted my story to help others. And even though it sounds clichéd, I believed that if one person didn't give up on their life because of me, then it would be worth it.

A cancer diagnosis comes with a lot of rethinking and reflecting. I did that, too. The grief over losing your previous life is persistent and recurrent. It infiltrates everything: your sense of self, your relationships, your career, everything. I have known many women who were abandoned by their husbands or boyfriends after cancer. Part of recovery is gluing together the fragmented pieces of your past life into something new.

After I finished purging the closet, I felt lighter, better. So I decided to examine my life and clean out anything else that was weighing it down. For me, that meant getting rid of toxic relationships. I used to have a patient with schizophrenia who talked about "energy vampires" that followed him around. I believe we all have energy vampires in our lives whose sole purpose is to drain our life force. They can be more malignant than cancer. When in a crisis though, it's important to weed them out. That's what I ended up doing. All those who thought my cancer was really about them carried no place in my life. As those chains broke, I found myself free to share more of me with the world. I kept writing my blog, I was chosen to be the Ford Warrior in Pink; I was picked to do a fund raising commercial. I gave my story to the world and in return, I got a community of women and men who could relate to my struggles and take courage from my fight. I feel like I won this bargain.

I want to go, as I am, with my personality, my memories, myself intact. My husband knows I am me because of my brain.

34

SEE SPOT RUN

A parking spot in the city is almost a divine gift; a spot on a shirt can be a nuisance; a new breakfast spot is awesome. But when a spot is on the MRI of your brain, it can change the trajectory of your life.

There is a spot on the MRI of my brain, deep in the brain. "A lesion" as the radiologist called it in his report. They see something "enhancing" on the MRI. Perhaps it is hope lighting up or the proverbial light bulb going off. It's a "small lesion," the convenient medical word for a "thingee" that's not supposed to be there.

So the MRI found a "thingee" in my brain, but in the purgatory of radiological reporting, they can't decide what this means. "Rule out" is one of the favorite phrases when it comes to diagnostic inadequacies. "Cannot rule out" is even lamer.

While reading the report, my eyes focus on the line "Cannot rule out dural metastasis." Metastasis, a word that haunts every cancer survivor.

I breathe.

They see an enhancing lesion in the brain. Just to balance the sentence, they throw in "could be a vein." Could be a vein, meningioma, or dural metastasis.

Anyone want to throw darts here?

Things move slowly. I try to focus on what my thought was before I read the report on my phone as I was rushing out the door to take my daughter to school and head to work after. She, I realize, is pulling on my hand to get going.

I read the report again: It's not normal. Yesterday, I was told it was normal and I had already done my dance of joy. Today was supposed to be the blissful day after. But it is not. Because there is this spot.

Breast cancer can spread to other organs and seems to favor the liver, bones, and brain.

My worst fear since the diagnosis is that it would hit my brain. My brain is what I do, what I feel, what I bring to the table. It's who I am. My brain defines who I am.

That brain has a spot on it.

I was anxious about the MRI anyways. When tests happen, things get found.

Artifacts look good in a museum, but horrible in a CT of the liver, especially in a cancer patient. I have had an artifact in the liver CT. It did a disappearing act in the MRI (or the prayers washed off the artifact, or the radiologist was tired).

Things show up on imaging. When you have had cancer, an incidental finding is a finding no one wants to take lightly. An appointment with the neuro-oncology department follows.

"We are obviously worried this may be a tumor," was the doctor's opening statement.

Brain tumor? My mind goes blank.

"We can't be certain what it is."

Keep talking…

"Are you having any symptoms?"

The MRI was ordered after a five-day migraine that wouldn't go away with Imitrex. After suffering for five days, I opted to see the doctor. I knew this would get kicked up to "must see a neurologist" and what will a neurologist do with a cancer patient who is having a long, drawn-out headache?

Yeah, you guessed it, brain MRI.

The headache went away but left me with a gift of the spot.

Not too long ago, I had a casual chat with a cardiologist about the status of my heart and how chemotherapy can have long-term effects. I was worrying about my heart.

But this is the brain, the small organ that is in charge. When it gets inflamed, there is no room for swelling to go. Small, squiggly, soft, squishy brain that holds all of me in it.

I thought of the lady I had met in the radiation suite, whose face was half paralyzed with a brain tumor being irradiated. She had such a void in her eyes, but they still filled up with tears while talking to me.

It's a deep lesion. I understand as a physician that it cannot be accessed by a needle. I don't want a needle in my brain anyway. No one does.

Lots of thoughts gather in my brain along with the spot.

I have had conversations with my husband on this topic and they all end with this conclusion: "If it's in the brain, I am not doing anything."

I want to go, as I am, with my personality, my memories, myself intact. My husband knows it's my worst fear, and it has been since diagnosis. He knows I am me because of my brain.

Now there are second opinions to be had and films to be reviewed and then, the "wait and watch."

So here it is, the spot and me.

The feeling of being stuck has dogged me since I was diagnosed with breast cancer in 2013.

I have been trying to escape this patient role ever since, but it turns out the patient trumped the doctor.

35

DREAM

I feel utterly helpless. The coat is heavy on my shoulders, its pockets full of stuff: a flashlight, a tendon hammer, measuring tape, small pharmacopeia, a little file, and numerous pens. I stand at the nursing station and desperately ask the nurse to show me how to call the unit I got paged from. But they ignore me completely, chatting and charting, charting and chatting. I feel hot and nervous. My on-call pager keeps buzzing with numbers that I don't recognize but somehow feel that they are coming from the ICU. My call is starting, they need to talk to me, but I have no idea how to call these numbers.

Horrible scenarios play in my mind of someone being coded and my resident looking for the intern on call. My pager buzzes again. I am desperate. I suddenly notice this hospital unit is different. It has no windows or doors. I realize the walls are too high and there are no exits. I imagine the shame and humiliation of being the intern who went missing, the intern who did not respond to emergencies, and a doctor who let patients suffer on her call. I am immersed in the anxiety of being irresponsible and unavailable.

With sudden panic, I wake up in my bed, drenched in sweat. I realize that I was an intern about twenty years ago. The experienced psychiatrist in me starts to rapidly analyze the dream.

Anxiety, stuck, no control, intern—seems pretty clear.

The feeling of being stuck has dogged me since I was diagnosed with breast cancer in 2013. I have been trying to escape this patient role ever since, but it turns out the patient trumped the doctor.

I am now a professional patient. I'm experienced in surgeries, anesthesia routines, assisting the phlebotomists in finding my veins, and other mundane things that one acquires after a prolonged time spent wandering the hallways of a big medical center. I am really good at picking out the newly diagnosed patients at the cancer center. They always have this awful dread on their face as if they're watching themselves in a horror movie. They are the ones who look lost and reach for all the handouts in the waiting rooms. Veterans like me have them memorized. There are pamphlets for seminars on how to draw the brows right, how to battle fatigue, how to create a nutritious diet, and how to join ongoing studies and trials. When I see anyone carefully scanning those, I know there's a new recruit to the cancer world. The newbies also expect to be seen on time. What they don't know yet is that waiting is now a major part of their life. Waiting for results, waiting for scans, waiting for appointments, waiting for life to happen.

They will learn gradually just as I did. They will worry less about these things after a year.

About twenty years ago in January, I was standing with my luggage at the Greyhound station in New York City. It was late in the evening and I was new to America. I had been warned that this is an unsafe area and that I should not leave the Greyhound station. Growing up in Pakistan, I had hardly ever gone anywhere alone. Nonetheless, I found myself standing at the Port Authority Bus Terminal waiting for a friend to pick me up. While trying to stay inconspicuous, I observed the interesting characters around me. I watched a woman in a short red skirt and fishnet stockings smoke like a chimney, a man in a wheelchair seeking someone to buy a ticket for him, and hundreds of other people rushing past.

I was scared, unsure what to do if my ride fell through. Dressed in a secondhand winter coat bought from a resale bazaar in Karachi, I imagined I looked pretty tough. The truth is, however, a twenty-something petite female in a business suit clutching a giant suitcase doesn't inspire much fear in the hard-edged residents of NYC. Nevertheless, I stood there like I wasn't afraid.

I had arrived here after a grueling visa process to interview for a psychiatry residency. Lucky enough to have several interview appointments, I was traveling to hospitals all over the country. I had heard about America of course, and seen it in movies, but I had lived a pretty sheltered life until that point and had no idea what to anticipate. Sometimes I look back in amazement. What the heck was I thinking standing alone at 10:00 p.m. in the NYC Port Authority Terminal surrounded by sketchy characters? But back then nothing mattered. I was here with one goal, to become an American-trained psychiatrist. I graduated from one of the most prestigious universities in Pakistan, I wasn't going let anything come between me and my dream.

I somehow managed to deflect all marriage proposals that would curb my career in medicine. I was not going to marry anyone who would stifle my efforts. In my heart, I was skeptical of traditional arranged marriages. I had seen many women doctors find good spouses and become stay-at-home moms. I doubt all of them would have made that choice if they knew what they were getting into from the start. So I eschewed the traditional route and chased my career across the world...in the process meeting a fellow psychiatrist who supported my ambitions every step of the way. In spite of my current situation, I feel fortunate.

At six now, she
still worries about
monsters under
the bed, while the
scariest monster
that stalks her life,
lives within me.

36

MOMMY AND THE BEAST

Tomorrow she will graduate from kindergarten. I will be thankful that I was there, present in my mortal body, for at least one graduation of hers. There will be no gowns or hats, and she won't know what this moment means to me, but that is just fine. She is excited about wearing her pretty beaded dress and singing the "Good-Bye Song." I am planning not to wear mascara and to use a waterproof eyeliner. I will drag myself to get dressed no matter how exhausted I am from chemotherapy. I will take some Imodium so I can last through the ninetyminutes without rushing to the restroom.

She has been preparing the songs they will sing at this celebration they call "The Spring Sing" their school's annual tradition. She has her daddy's strong vocal cords and when she sings "America the Beautiful." you can't help but feel patriotic. She also has her father's loud laugh, which warms my heart, but thankfully her ability to carry a tune from her mom. I have voice memos on my phone of this spontaneous and joyful laugh for my dark days—living with cancer, I am guaranteed many.

She is a happy six-year-old who doesn't like sad endings or goodbyes. Come to think of it, nobody does, but at this age, she also does not comprehend them fully. She doesn't get the finality of death but can be very dramatic if I say, "Mommy doesn't feel well."

She will ask, "So are you going to DIE?"

Kids this age often become curious about death, although they're too young to grasp it. She cannot fully comprehend the fact that her mother is exactly one week out from her chemotherapy for metastatic breast cancer, which after almost a year of stability, suddenly became turbo charged.

She was two-and-half years old when cancer entered her mother's life and hers. She has grown up in the last four years under the lingering shadow of illness although she still calls it "Breath Cancer" perhaps not too inaccurate as eventually it's the breath that succumbs to this disease. She has grown up seeing pink ribbons in her house, and she identifies them as "therapy," a broken word she picked up somewhere along the endless conversations of chemotherapy, therapy, and radiation therapy. Never mind that she is the daughter of two psychiatrists, "therapy" has been a big part of her life.

But she prefers purple over pink. And I nurture that preference.

I want her as far from pink as possible even though the burden of my pink will accompany her all her life. This instills such guilt in me. I sometimes stare at her as I bathe her, thinking to myself, *I hope her body doesn't betray her.* I wrap all the guilt gently in my heart and do the best I can.

A few weekends ago, she and I watched *Beauty and the Beast.* She was enchanted by the movie until they had to abandon Belle's mother. As soon as the movie ended, she went on a tirade about why that happened and I had to give her meek explanations which would exonerate the mother from this terrible act of being sick and dying.

This reminded me of when we watched *Kung Fu Panda* several years ago and the mother panda sacrificed herself to save her cub. That evening she went to bed sobbing, explaining to me over and over that "Leaving your baby is not a good thing for a mommy to do!"

I tried to put my psychiatrist hat on and talked her out of her grief. I had assumed she would forget about it the next day, but no, she cornered me in the kitchen.

"Why did she leave her baby? Mommies are not supposed to do that!"

I remember I decided to take an art therapy approach with her. I sat her down and we drew pictures of the panda family which needed to be a complete family: Mom, Dad, and their child. Pretty soon, she voiced how she was mad at the Daddy for not protecting the Mommy and baby. I roped my husband into our little art session. He had to draw some pandas as well. We tried to restore the trust of her complete family unit. During her toddlerhood, she was obsessed with Diego and his animals finding their mothers. At some level, she has internalized the anxiety that plagues our home.

At six now, she still worries about monsters under the bed, while the scariest monster that stalks her life, lives within me.

My boy was six when I was first diagnosed; now my girl is the same age. She will graduate kindergarten, just like my boy did two months before my very first diagnosis.

I clearly remember my life at that time. I was working and busy. I felt fat at 130 pounds and complained that my dress showed too much pudge. I remember being upset that my long shiny thick hair wasn't behaving and looked frizzy and that I didn't have the time to get it done. I had a curious six-year-old and a two-year-old who battled potty training. Everything was rushed and stressful.

But those times were the really the good times. I was healthy, strong, and working. I was a successful doctor and a Mom. But I was not treating myself with compassion. I had too many demons in my mind, the perfections and the *should-be's* that were getting in the way of appreciating my beautiful life.

Four years later, living with cancer, I'm a different person. I have greatly unloaded stress. I have embraced self-compassion and my vulnerabilities. I am kinder to myself and allow myself to be "good enough" as opposed to "perfect." Tomorrow, I will be thankful that I still have my own hair for the graduation (it will likely fall out in another few weeks) and that I get to see another day.

I am no longer the neurotic mother I used to be, preoccupied with developmental milestones, extracurricular classes, and the kids' academic future. I am more of a "here and now" mom. I resigned from my practice to be more available to my kids. Cancer has changed the mother in me. I understand there is nothing perfect about motherhood. In fact, motherhood is full of shortcomings, but they can be compensated by a loving heart. I reassure myself that Beauty did eventually find happiness in her life.

In my life, the petals keep falling. But I have to keep faith that magic can happen sometimes.

Both a little scared, neither one prepared, Mommy and the Beast.

37

UP IN THE AIR

The wheels of the pulley are rolling and I am floating up gradually. The Florida sun is strong and the sky is clear. The whole scene is drenched in different shades of blue. I am clipped onto a harness that is slowly rising up into the sky and a bright purple and orange parachute is providing the adequate pull to my son and me. I recall sitting in the boat a few minutes ago as the staff of the parasailing company asked me to put on a life jacket, and I am about to bow out from this experience when my inner voice tells me, *It's now or never!* Cancer has beaten me into giving up control and surrendering, so now I seldom get in my own way.

And just like that I am locked into a harness and hanging over the ocean. I'm holding the harness so tightly that my arms hurt and I tell myself *This should not be so painful.* My son is getting anxious even though he has prior experience, and I try to act tough for him. I remind myself that I am making memories. He should not remember this experience as "Mommy was so scared" when I am gone. I even smile.

I make myself look up and around at the view which is simply gorgeous. I see white sandy beaches and a widespread ocean with shops and restaurants and boats on the coast of Destin. I allow myself to relax and embrace the moment. I surrender to the wind and breathe.

The wind is gently blowing and the parachute sways a little, it's a nice slow movement, and to me it feels akin to what an unborn child might experience in the womb. A rope runs from the parachute all the way down to the boat. I wonder if this what it feels like when the spirit leaves the body, slowly floating up to escape.

I gradually warm up to this ride and actually feel a great sense of accomplishment because I am parasailing. My daughter and husband are waving at us from the boat. I manage a short quick wave back and then grasp the harness again.

A week later, I'm laying on a gurney in a hospital gown.

The green gown with its hideous print is too large for me, but still somehow too skimpy to cover my butt because the flaps don't tie in the right place. The nakedness makes me even more vulnerable.

I had been in the ER for incessant pain, nausea, and vomiting for two days before it was determined that the cancer had eroded my skull bone, causing severe pressure on my brain. My biggest fear after my cancer metastasized was brain involvement, and there I was with a five centimeter growth in my skull. It required a craniotomy.

Craniotomy is the medical term for cutting the skull open. Yes, that sacred space of the body that guards my identity, the essential "me," was going to be cut open.

After having gone through numerous surgeries since my first diagnosis of breast cancer in July 2013, I know the precise instant that I hate the most about any surgery. It's those first few inescapable moments in the recovery room when a nurse is screaming (or what feels like screaming) in my ear as she shakes me vigorously, "Uzma! Uzma! Your surgery is over, you are waking up now." That first moment of awareness brings with it a strong wave of pain, and I try to estimate how much pain these buggers have left me in. Waking up from mastectomy and liver ablation were horrifying and excruciatingly painful, but I have no idea what it would be like to wake up from a craniotomy.

The anesthesiologist shows up and waves a syringe filled with few CCs of an orange liquid, "Versed" she says. It's the happy medicine. The psychiatrist in me feels a little offended at this turf encroachment, since I am the one who usually prescribes happy medicine. She asks for my name and date of birth for the umpteenth time, and I respond like a smart student. I don't tolerate Versed in the sense that I fall asleep after getting it intravenously and never get the moments of giddy disinhibition, unlike other patients who have some tolerance. Things are beeping around me, and I am covered with a blanket. I know that pretty soon it's light out and I vaguely remember my husband kissing me as I get wheeled to the OR. The wheels of the gurney start to move.

I'm in the OR and there's a mask on my face. Someone is asking me to breathe deeply. I try to say, " I know what you are doing to me!" but no words come out. The grip of the mask on my face and the pressure of the the anesthesiologist's hand on top of it gets stronger. I look up at the OR lights. The happy medicine is working.

I assume I sleep until that moment in the recovery comes. However this time, it will be a moment I remember for the rest of my life, however short it might be, as joyful.

Two nurses are speaking among themselves as I am waking from the deep slumber, "What is the neurological deficit?" a fair question to ask about anyone who has had their skull cut open by a neurosurgeon for three hours.

The other voice responds, "None."

I am glad to be awake.

There is no deficit.

Exactly one week earlier I was floating in the sky, and now I'm in the ICU with lines running back and forth and I/Vs poking me, compression stockings on my legs, and my head in severe post-op pain, the bandages hiding a five-inch scar on the back of my head. My metastatic breast cancer progressed but my bucket list has gotten shorter and there is no deficit. Only fulfillment.

Dear Dad,
You won the
death race and
dodged your
daughter's
funeral.

You collected
happy memories
in your blanket
and coffin.

38

THE LAST DAY

Daddy, this is Uzma!"

It's the first time I needed to do that. Never in his eighty-seven years had I needed to introduce myself to the man who introduced me to the world in all its amazing ways. Ironic that I needed to remind him who I was on the last day of his life.

My entrance didn't elicit a reaction. No movement, no gesture, no smile. I had seen him just two days ago, and he had told me, "Come back soon, okay?" I had nodded in affirmation. He was up in his room and I, chronically tired by chemotherapy, didn't have the energy to go up the flight of stairs to hug him once more. I didn't know then that I had passed up the chance for a last hug with my father.

A disruptive respiratory sound of accumulated mucus was audible from his throat, the liquid spinning in a chaotic fashion in a pipe that connected to the ventilator. It took a little while to get accustomed to that sound and accept it as part of the impending death. The phrase "death rattle" is actually used in medicine. That sound was indeed the death rattle.

The hospice nurse used tiny lollipop-like sponges to keep his mouth wet, and periodically his lips would pucker around it. He had largely stopped swallowing by then, but my mom, in her desire to feed him his favorite food, kept bringing bowls of strawberry ice cream in the vain hope that he would be able to enjoy it. She remained interested in extending his life even though that morning arrangements for a funeral and grave were being made.

A strange mismatch of acceptance and denial often plays out in deaths. Even when we can hear it and see it, we choose not to. I was also torn. The physician in me knew before hopping on a train from Chicago to Milwaukee that I am going to visit a dying man. But as soon as I entered the room, a daughter's tears flooded my eyes. I regrouped myself to assess the seriousness of this juncture in his life. The death rattle often lasts no more than twenty-four to forty-eight hours. I had packed clothes for a day. I positioned myself right next to him in his bed.

Given my own Stage IV metastatic breast cancer, I have read plenty articles on death, dying, and the transition.

Keenly aware that hearing is maintained util the last moments, I used this chance to express my love for him. I played some of his favorite qawwali (devotional) music and would see his toes move. I can no longer hear those songs now without bawling.

I asked him for a selfie and I got an awkward facial movement that could be considered the best smile from a dying man, or so I decided to believe.

His eyes had started to look muddied. The hospice nurse explained it was an imminent sign. I stuck even closer to him. It was the last few hours to cuddle with Dad and I wasn't letting those go. His grip on my hand remained firm until the end even as his grip was loosening over life. I stroked his hair, and he passed away with more hair than I currently have. My own image of death has always been dying bald, without eyebrows and lashes, I felt happy that he had been spared the indignity.

He used to sleep with a comb at his bedside and if woken up, he would comb his air into place, then fall back asleep. He never looked shabby. He also had very sharp hearing, much like mine. During my medical school training, when I woke up at 2:00 a.m. to study, he would gently call me from the bedroom with one eye open and ask, "Are you making tea?" That question incorporated the assumption that he gets a cup too.

> I asked him for a selfie and I got an awkward facial movement that could be considered the best smile from a dying man or so I decided to believe.

He would drink that cup and then immediately fall asleep. I would envy his sleep which remained terrific until he started taking steroids for his lung disease. He was an early sleeper and early riser, and I suspect it was a significant factor in his mental sharpness up until some delirium set in his final days.

For the last five years, Dad had very tactfully avoided my cancer and diligently tried to convince me that the next scan would be normal. He needed to say this aloud to make it believable. I would fall a little into his denial hope trap, too. Then scan results would come and he would reset expectations to the future scan. I had suspected that internally he knew that I was terminal, and he had decided that he would go before me. His decline began right after I got diagnosed with metastatic disease. He became more desperate, vague, and in denial during my illness.

When I got cancer, it took me a while to hear my voice saying "I have cancer." I thought it was the hardest thing to say. Little did I realize that saying "My Daddy passed away" would be so much worse. I am currently trying to work past the denial that I will never see him again, never call him when I want to talk. I will never see his pride in his grandchildren. I will never hear him say the fatiha prayers for his only daughter.

Dear Dad,

You won the death race and dodged your daughter's funeral. You collected happy memories in your blanket and coffin. I hope they offered you the same ease when your last breath was leaving your chest, and I woefully wish for a similar peaceful death, in my own bed and blanket surrounded by loving family.

You are no longer here, but you're within me, in my choices, my desires, my present, and my future. This Father's Day I will celebrate your legacy within me. I will celebrate the life that came from yours.

39

THE FUTURE

Ever since I got diagnosed with metastatic breast cancer, I hear this phrase a lot: "Well, no one really knows how long he or she has to live."

True, no one does. I nod in agreement.

Mostly the phrase is said to be kind or polite because people don't know what to say to someone in my situation. They know very well in their hearts that the odds of me getting old and seeing my grandkids are much lower than theirs. That is the harsh reality.

Yes, no one knows how long they've got to live, but how many think about dying every day?

My typical day involves hearing about someone's disease progressing, about someone getting whole brain radiation, about someone passing on from the same illness that plagues me. I have two choices: either pretend that "they" are not "me," and I will be different, or realize that this could be me and spend each day mindfully.

I go back and forth between these two options. There are good days full of temporary hope, and there are days that haunt me. Those are the days I live in fear. What if today my treatment stops working? Thinking about death and dying is considered morbid by those who don't have a terminal illness. People who think about death are "negative people."

The reality is that those who are healthy do not live life in full view of death. They may sometimes get a moment or two when they reflect about life's unpredictability, but then they return to the bliss of not having to confront it. Those with metastasis cannot turn off the thought that death is nearby, like an exasperating next-door neighbor. This isn't me being macabre; it's just my reality. The life expectancy and mortality rates related to my illness are real statistics; they're not manufactured or grabbed out of thin air.

I wish for a long survival, but I can't deny what is happening in my body right now. My cancer sleeps with me and wakes up with me every day. Last week, a friend of mine was urging my classmates to buy a lifetime membership to an association. I doubt anyone else besides me did the math of whether I will break even or not if I invest. A yearly membership is $90, a lifetime membership is $500, which meant I needed to live six years to profit from the lifetime offer. Will I? Who knows? But if you were in my situation, would you write that check?

A month ago, while I was shopping for eyeliner, a lovely makeup artist tried to sell me eyebrow powder and said, "This will last you at least three years." I smiled and wondered if I would outlast the eyebrow powder.

People like to plan on a "someday." As in, "Someday, I will _____" (fill in the blank with a dream or goal). For me, the luxury of "someday" has disappeared. My someday is today. So next time you meet a cancer survivor and have the urge to say "life is not guaranteed for anyone," think of all the things you did that day with your future in mind (be it contributing to a 401(k) or planning a birthday party). Reflect on what changes you would make in your life if suddenly your tomorrow wasn't guaranteed.

Dare I say that it would be exhausting to consider that in a month you might be no more, and live every day as if it were your last? How long can anyone without a terminal illness willingly do that?

Thinking about the end isn't putting life on hold but rather reflecting to make it more meaningful. My life isn't on hold either; it's moving forward, and yes, I might even outlive some of you. But people bet money in a gamble only when the odds of winning are high. My odds are low; you know that and I know that.

That's how life is played, based on odds. All I know is today. Today I live on, despite of what is inside me.

I want know what death is like, but no one wants to talk to me about it. I have Stage IV incurable cancer, so death is one of the possibilities (to be fair, isn't it a surety for us all?) but no one says anything. Not my oncologist, not my internist. I have no partner in the internal dialogue I have with myself.

I have this black and white image of me in a hospital bed, with a morphine drip in my arm. I see big windows. Based on what I know about the ruthlessness of terminal cancer, I see myself pale and emaciated. I have a headscarf, no hair, no eyebrows, no eyelashes, and a weak forced on smile on my ashen face.

I imagine the moment it will be over. Will it be when my kids are teenagers? Or will it be sooner while they're still young and don't really understand death? But then again, who understands death anyways? I often read articles about death and dying. I am curious about the actual process. I wonder if it hurts when the soul leaves the body. Is it ripped out violently or is it a gentle release of breath?

As a doctor, I have seen death many times. I have felt its presence in the room. I have seen it in the heart monitor decline and in the sweat of the doctor pumping the chest of someone he knows will never wake up. I am an acquaintance of death but with cancer, it's become a friendship. Death is my tantalizing mysterious friend who hangs out around me, looking for me to embrace it. Cancer has marked me and introduced me to death. The introduction was awkward. I was mad at cancer for bringing this friend along but as my fears and anxiety dissipated, I became curious about this ever-present ending of the show we call life.

When I was young, I often thought about which kind of death is easier: sudden unknowing death or a prolonged suffering leading to the inevitable. I always favored the latter because I am a planner. An impending knowing death provides an opportunity to contemplate, reflect, and make amends. It seems that death has heard my thoughts and I have been granted my choice.

I have seen sudden deaths. The first death I witnessed in my professional training was in the ER. A seven-year-old girl was rushed in with a gunshot wound that went through her neck. The carotid artery was spraying blood everywhere. In spite of the chaos and commotion, an entire team of doctors came together to save her. I was stunned, scared, and amazed all at once. I thought they would manage it. Then I saw the heart rate slowly plummet, a downward spiral as she slipped into the waiting arms of death. The voice of the senior ER resident still echoes in my ears:

"Get her mother to sit in one of the counseling rooms."

I understood what that meant.

Soon someone was mopping the floor where puddles of blood collected and I heard screams from the counseling room.

"Dying" is a frivolous word. Technically, we are all dying since we all do eventually. I suppose the word indicates one's proximity to the end. Although in my opinion living supersedes dying the closer you are to death. Living is a long, arduous, and adventurous process. Dying is not living. Dying is living poorly. Dying leads to death also but reflects a lot more misery in approaching death. I don't believe in dying. Only in living and death.

Life is meant to be carved out of death and its eventuality. Death is forever while life is finite. That is why living is much harder because it requires sustained effort. Death is a final verdict without any second chances, whereas life is a long opportunity to redo. The circulating blood in the body is continuously fighting against death; so is the pumping heart. The neurons in the brain keep firing electricity through an intricate network, all with the goal of keeping the lights on.

Living, therefore, requires tremendous practice and awareness. Living needs to be conscious because the force that opposes it needs just one chance. Living is an uphill battle, an exercise in tenacity. Living requires hope and will.

I am constantly amazed by the human body, its ability to grow and thrive, sometimes methodical and resolute and sometimes chaotic and rogue.

40

MY EXTRAORDINARY BODY

She puts the ultrasound gel on my belly, squirting the warm sticky blue goo from the bottle as she stares at the screen of her machine. The transducer "wand" is pressed against my liver, the focus of this test. The sensation takes me back ten years and I recall my obstetrician doing the same thing. Then, the focus was a little lower. I remember the same gel, the same wand, the doctor fidgeting with the equipment, then a gurgling sound coming out of the machine as the OB smiled and said, "There is your washing machine." It was the heartbeat of my first child and my heart filled with pure joy.

Today's procedure was essentially the same, but there would be no washing machine sound, no smiles. This time the doctor was looking for a growth, but not a welcome one.

I am constantly amazed by the human body, its ability to grow and thrive, sometimes methodical and resolute and sometimes chaotic and rogue. My body has grown two healthy babies, gallstones, and cancer. It is remarkable. I have experienced the magic of birth and how the entire body synchronizes to accomplish this goal. I used to think about it often in medical school, especially during embryology class when I learned the intricate details of human fetal development. I would think, "So much could go wrong, and yet, most of the time, it doesn't." The more I learned about it, the more it amazed me. The muscles and joints, the complex organ systems, the 206 bones, they all combine to create the most fascinating apparatus in nature. But the mysteries of the human brain intrigued me the most. The biological rhythms of the body, the sleep and wake cycle, and even the ticking of the biological clock. Every medical textbook I read (anatomy, physiology, embryology) made me more and more in awe of the human body.

And then one day, something very wrong happened within my extraordinary body. A few cells with a mind of their own started to proliferate. The shock of this new behavior was overwhelming but at the same time I believe in the resilience of my body. After all, this the habitat where my soul resides. This is where my heart beats to keep me alive. It is full of internal mechanisms that save and protect me and have for years on end. During residency, when I was on call for 36 hours straight running back and forth between floors on aching legs, my body obliged. When I went without meals for hours to help patients one after the next with my stomach gurgling, my body delivered. The endless nights in the ER, pumped full of caffeine and adrenaline, my body and mind worked together. My body fought viruses, bacteria, and a whole host of other invaders successfully…until now.

Many cancer patients feel that their body betrayed them. It's a very popular theme with people who write or speak about cancer. However, I disagree. The fact is that from the moment of conception, all the human body knows is growth. It starts as just a few cells and grows into a fetus, then into a toddler, then an adult. Growth is the body's primary function for decades. Granted, cancer growth is damaging and haphazard, but how can I blame the body?

Having cancer doesn't mean that I am all cancer. There are many healthy parts of me still working efficiently (even in spite of the chemotherapy chemicals that have saturated my organs for years). Cancer is part of the conglomerate of cells that I carry, but I am not walking and talking cancer. It may take over most of my cells one day, but I will never hate my body for it, not even my breasts, the source of the rogue cells. My breasts once carried the capacity to nourish two infants and I will be forever grateful to them.

In my opinion, there is nothing more resilient than a human body. It can function without ovaries, a gallbladder, or an appendix, and with just one kidney. It has an amazing capacity to self-heal. Most people will stop bleeding on their own, get better from viral illnesses, and can overcome a broken rib without medical intervention. The body fights and survives until its last moments and that is where I find the most hope.

Cancer is a brutal
teacher who doesn't
allow much practice. You
have to stay on your toes
all the time because
the curveballs
are frequent.

41

SURVIVOR

I have started to wonder how resilient I truly am. I keep falling and getting up. It has been a long road since July 2013 when cancer first hit and knocked over my life. The relationships, the children, the career, the marriage, all thrashed about as if in a storm. I have spent the last five years putting the pieces back together in the best way I could. Some pieces were no longer fitting, so I threw them away and some pieces are missing, so there are big gaping holes. I live my life between the hospital and the home. My third location of the office no longer exists as now I am an out of work psychiatrist. I like to introduce myself as a writer, an identity that started as a desperate attempt to cope with the onslaught of emotions, but then took on a life of its own. I literally have a fan following now. I get well-wishes and prayers from all over the world which is rather intoxicating. The buzz often works as lidocaine on my wounds and the cracks in my armor that deepen with the constant assaults of this vicious disease.

I had decided before I was diagnosed with metastatic disease that if (or when) I make it to my five-year cancer anniversary, I will go to New York City and shout that I am cancer-free from the middle of Times Square.

I made the wrong vow. Over these five years I have discovered that life needs to be celebrated on its own terms and conditions. And some restrictions do apply. I have those.

I know it's cliché, but appreciation of life only comes after things go wrong. Humans don't see anything clearly without contrast—we need the bad to appreciate the good, and vice versa. We try to protect ourselves but no one is immune to the calamities of life. It's what we do after we get hit that matters.

I have gotten hit twice and the second blow was a hard one. It suspended me between life and death in perpetuity. I feel banged up and tired, but I don't know what choice I have other than to fight back and claim from life what I deserve. As I calculate my survival based on what I know, I feel safe planning for a year. No more than that. I quietly calculate the ages of my kids and come up with the answer: still too young.

What is a metastatic woman to do? There is no cure, only ways to extend life. I can see the thought bubble above your head: "No, you will beat this. If anyone can, you can!" Well, thank you for this vote of confidence. Unfortunately I see women like me dying every day. Maybe my estimations are flawed, as I am not factoring miracles in my equation. But I am unsure why I would be granted one. If it happens, believe me I will take it. However, if you're relying on a miracle, you already know you are in deep shit. Perhaps that's why it feels farther and farther from my reach. Modern science seems to be far behind religion in miracle-making. Nonetheless, I will take it in any form, manmade or divine. Until that happens, I reach for the motivation and strength to go on—each day is my tiny miracle. Maybe over time they will add up to something meaningful. Or maybe not. The jury is out, and I wait.

Cancer is a brutal teacher who doesn't allow much practice. You have to stay on your toes all the time because the curveballs are frequent. I did not expect a craniotomy six weeks after a glorious vacation; neither did I expect the cancer to mutate and transform over three months to change its receptors. My life is life on quicksand. The moment you relax, it gets you, one way or the other. Some days it grabs you by the emotions and thrashes you around as you gasp and panic, feeling claustrophobic and fighting to breathe. Some days it robs you of sleep, and the anthem of failure and death plays slowly and rhythmically in your head. You walk into a blind tunnel on the faith that this will end somewhere.

It has been five years that I have been walking. I have seen flickers of light but also overpowering darkness. I am amazed sometimes that I haven't just banged my head on the tunnel walls until it bled to a silence.

I am walking. I no longer know what my destination is, but it seems the stopping makes the tunnel feel longer and colder.

I win because
although the scans,
the meds, the side effects,
the fears, the grief, the loss,
and the disability are
all part of my life, they
are NOT my life.

42

I AM TODAY

Hello there, my doppelgänger cells! Yeah you, the rogue bunch. Next week, we will find out what you're up to. But today, I win.

- I win as I celebrate one more rotation of the Earth and one more year of my life.
- I win for a year well lived.
- I win for all the things I did.
- I win for every day I looked at fear and said, "Fuck you!"
- I win for every time I hugged the newly diagnosed woman as she wept in my arms.
- I win because I went to bed in the arms of my loving husband.
- I win because my friendships are stronger than ever before.
- I win because I am loved.
- I win because I made it to my kids' school every time parents were supposed to.
- I win because despite the hurt, my heart has love beyond any mutation you can possibly create.
- I win because I reach out to all.
- I win because I make mistakes and I learn from them.

- I win because I keep fighting.
- I win because I do cry, but then I wipe my tears, get up, and live some more.

I win because although the scans, the meds, the side effects, the fears, the grief, the loss, and the disability are all part of my life, they are NOT my life.

I am my life, the whole canvas with the beautiful and the ugly.

I am today!

I am today!